Be a Better Manager

In Five Minutes a Day

By Dr Dominic McLoughlin

Title: Be a Better Manager in Five Minutes a Day
Copyright © 2022 by Dominic J. McLoughlin
https://dominicmcloughlin.com/
Illustrations by Georgia Behan-Smith

All rights reserved

ISBN: 978-0-9924872-4-9 (Paperback)
ISBN: 978-0-9924872-5-6 (Hardback)

Published by:
Ithikos Pty Ltd
Suite 124, Shop 19
150 Great Western Highway
Blaxland NSW 2774

ITHIKOS

Acknowledgements

I am very grateful for the help I received in producing this book. Lukas provided encouragement, feedback, and ongoing support. Natalie, the chief editor, provided ongoing editing and feedback. Craig provided comprehensive structural and line editing with very useful suggestions. Bill, Mark and Nick provided reader feedback while Paul reminded me of the details of some stories. Pip helped with the stories. Georgia provided the wonderful illustrations.

Writing this book embodied some of the ideas I am trying to outline. Lukas was practicing his life coaching skills and, at the same time, encouraging me to continue this project. Georgia was starting out as a recent graduate in animation and Craig was starting his editing. They all gave selflessly of their time and effort to produce something that would be of benefit to others.

To everyone who helped to see this project to a successful conclusion – thank you! I am very grateful.

FREE GIFT FOR MY READERS

How To Be a Better Manager - in JUST 5 Minutes a Day!

Get your Free Starter Kit here:
https://dominicmcloughlin.com/free-starter-kit/

Getting started is often the hardest part. However, as soon as you get going and the momentum kicks in, you can be unstoppable.

Therefore, I created this FREE Starter Kit to help you – in just 5 minutes a day!

Inside this FREE Starter Kit are:
- 5 tutorial videos
- 5 downloadable workbooks

Each Video has ideas for 5 minutes a day for one working week!

Find the answer to ALL the following people management questions:
- How do I find more time?
- How do I develop a manager's mindset?
- How do I build my people skills?
- How do I understand who my clients are?
- How do I build my team culture?

Over one month of ideas to help you improve!

Table of Contents

Introduction

In my first job, I was a difficult employee – I didn't mean to be – I was just a typical 18-year-old who thought he knew more than everyone else. What I find most interesting, looking back, is the different ways my managers and supervisors responded to me.

The supervisors

I was working in a blue collar, male dominated foundry – a big metal shed that was hot in summer and cold in winter. My supervisor in the 'store' was a middle-aged man who had worked there most of his life and was very clear about the way things should be done – his way.

One day, I was looking for a product that wasn't where he said it should be. It was my delight to point that out to him because he hadn't followed his own rules. It got heated. Very heated. After the accusations stopped flying, he said, "I can't fire you, but I can recommend you be fired." This was news to me, because until then I thought that he could in fact fire me – so the threat backfired. I now knew he was powerless.

This was an early lesson in the perils of using power and threats to try to manage people.

Another guy was the supervisor in the foundry area. He had a special brown uniform to separate him from us blue uniformed workers. All the important keys jangled loudly as he supervised. He also distributed the cash envelopes containing our pay. We crossed swords over something I can't even remember. In my adolescent wisdom, my response was never to reply to his 'good morning' again. I knew I was getting under his skin when a fellow worker said to me privately, "Come on – just say good morning to him." I had severely underestimated the effect of my behavior – I was poisoning what was actually a cohesive environment and unwittingly generating tension of which I was unaware. But everyone else was. My refusal to engage socially disrupted the team, harming the 'team spirit' that was wanted.

All was not lost, however. This first job caused me to reflect deeply and led to a sustained interest in how managers actually relate to people in their teams. This book is a result.

One thing this book seeks to explore is how we as managers can respond to the various team members and their behaviors – even difficult ones. Academics call the things outside of a job description 'organizational citizenship behavior' or 'discretionary behavior'. My 'good morning' example highlights the importance of discretionary behavior for a cohesive work environment and overall team dynamics. Here's one example of an alternative.

The Manager

My supervisor's boss was the manager – he really could fire me. I started very early in the morning and the CEO, who oversaw both my supervisor and his manager, was often the first to arrive. I took the opportunity to complain to him about a decision that my manager had made – I went over his head. The CEO yelled at me, telling me to get out and not bother him with such fiddling trifles ever again. Maybe that was what set the tone of the culture in that workplace.

However, my manager called me in to see him later that day and calmly explained that I had to accept a decision that he had made – it was final. He also explained that I had caused him trouble with the CEO, because he 'couldn't manage his staff'.

He took the time to speak to me privately. He pointed out that I had made a serious error and it had consequences – not just for me, but for others. In that instant, he gained my respect.

When I resigned at the end of that year to go to university (much to the relief of some, I am sure), that manager kindly gave me a written reference, recommending me to any future employer.

Since then, I have worked in many industries, from high conflict unionized environments to cutting edge IT companies. I have read and studied a lot. Synthesizing all the study and experience has resulted in this book, the aim of which is to answer a common question:

How can we inspire our team to achieve outstanding success?

The answers are relatively easy, but implementation is not. It is challenging, because to build a great environment for our team, we must first build up the trust our people have in us as managers. We have to be prepared to be a bit more vulnerable. A bit more curious about ourselves and others. We must work on our character.

For lasting, effective impact 'quick fixes', jargon and management techniques are not enough. Outstanding performance needs genuine trust, and we build this on the foundation of our own character. So, it is up to us.

Chapter 1:

Trust and Outstanding Performance

©dominicmcloughlin.com

In this Chapter:

- Why trust between managers and their team is crucial
- The business benefits
- The personal benefits
- How trust is built

Today, we've forgotten the impact of managers. However, we probably remember our favorite teacher, and of course, our worst. Depending on our age, we also probably remember our favorite boss, and our worst. Our favorite boss was probably our best boss. We remember how they made us feel about ourselves, our work and our colleagues. Our worst boss made our lives miserable – and we still remember that sinking feeling in our stomach when we had to face another day.

If you are reading this book, you are probably looking for ways to be a better manager. You want to be on the 'good boss' side of the management spectrum. But how? There are countless university degrees and diplomas telling you how. And yet, there are still managers who instill misery into their team. Why?

As managers, most of us want to have a happy workplace, but lots of things get in the way. Often, we haven't thought about *how* we manage. We tend to do things in the same way as when we were managed, or the way we *think* people should be managed. Maybe we are so used to thinking in terms of processes, or blinded by the sheer amount that needs to be done. We lose sight of our genuine interest in happiness and growth for ourselves and the people working for us.

Remember the best manager you ever had? What things did they do and what things didn't they do to hold this place in your memory? Were they efficient? Maybe. Did they make you want to come to work? Maybe. Was there something about them that inspired you? What was it? Maybe the key element was that you trusted them?

Overwhelmingly, people answer yes to this question about the best manager in terms of trust. Over time, we build up an assessment of that manager's behavior and motivations. We do this with everyone. Can I trust you? Will you have my back? Will you catch me if I fall? Managers are exposed to this scrutiny in a particularly public way. Much depends on the outcomes of such scrutiny.

Usually, starting with small things, people take a risk and build up an assessment of whether someone can be trusted.

If you want your team members to perform well, then you too, need to build trust. It is the crucial element for being a good manager.

Why is Trust Crucial?

Returning to that best manager you ever had. Were you comfortable to share information with them? Were you happy to say what was going on – good or bad? Were you happy to take advice and correction from them? If your answer is yes, then you trusted them. In this book, you will find suggestions for the behaviors that inspire your people to trust you.

Other important factors reveal more about the motivations of the best managers. Did that best manager help you in your career? Did they genuinely listen to you and consider your perspective? Were they concerned about you? Were you happy to put in that extra effort? I suspect you said yes to most, or all, of these questions too, because it reveals that the best managers are not just in it for themselves. They genuinely want to see their team members grow and succeed.

Why is trust so important? Because the manager sets the tone for the entire team. Both experience and research support this. How often to you hear of CEOs resigning because of an organization's poor performance? Was it poor performance, or poor management? In these cases, the common expressions 'people leave their boss, not their organization', or 'a fish rots from the head first' seem accurate. We will explore this in more detail in the following chapters.

Let's take a moment to consider a bad manager. Think of the worst manager you ever had. What was it like working there? Were you reluctant or afraid to go to work? Were you cautious about sharing ideas and information? Were you reluctant to put in the extra effort? Probably.

Don't get me wrong… fear works… for a while. That's why it is often the preferred management strategy for so many dysfunctional organizations. However, this is not an environment where people flourish and contribute their best efforts. The 'tone' that the manager sets is the foundation for the way the team members work together and treat each other. If you don't trust your colleagues and your manager, you will be reluctant to contribute any great ideas you have – because someone else will take the credit. You will be reluctant to put in any extra effort, as there is no guarantee someone will help you in return. All of this leads to a fear-based team culture, which inevitably leads to substandard performance over time.[1]

It is only in an environment of strong or high trust that managers can generate outstanding performance.

Trust is complicated because human relationships are complicated. People are messy, they're not composed of straight lines and sharply defined edges. When it comes to trusting a manager, human complexity and inconsistency make rapid, accurate assessment difficult. Past experience – good and bad, personal biases, issues in people's personal lives all contribute to how trust is going to develop. Trust requires a response from both parties. The good news is, we can all build trust – one step at a time. Because you set the tone for the people in your team, when people trust you, they are much more likely to trust each other, too.

Let's have a more detailed look at the benefits of strong trust – for the business, and for you.

Business Outcomes

Academic research over many years has established a strong connection between trust and managerial success which translates into benefits for the business. One highly regarded analysis by Dirks and Ferrin (2002) looked back over 40 years of trust research and examined 106 studies to draw out the key relationships.[2]

We can summarize the business benefits outlined in the study as the staff being:
- committed to the business goals,
- committed to the organization
- satisfied with their manager
- satisfied with their job
- prepared to believe the information that is shared with them
- happy in their role and not looking to leave.

These are all key fundamentals of outstanding performance.[3] If one of these was missing, sure, the team members could perform. But how well? Now compound this with every person in the team having one (or more) of these fundamentals missing. A recipe for long-term success? Clearly not.

As we have seen, a key benefit of trust in the manager and trust in team members is to encourage positive behaviors and interactions between people. Imagine the following:

You are in a team where everyone only does the things that are in their job description – and nothing else.

No one says good morning to each other, no one asks about how the weekend went. No one cares about making the targets, or about learning new things. The most common response to an enquiry is 'not my job, you'll have to ask someone else'. No socializing, no sharing of information. No one does anything to help a colleague.

Inspiring place to work? Probably not. Looking forward to Monday morning? Thanks, but no thanks.

Let's add the layers that operate in the background to freeze out any sense of team effort – absenteeism, for example. When all of your people are taking all of their sick leave every year, that is a lot of effort lost. Similarly – your people can be present in body, but absent in effort. Classic examples are 'playing solitaire' and 'checking social media' for hours of the day. Mind-numbing and demoralizing. But all too common.

Now let's look at the reverse situation – a team where everyone does their job, but goes above and beyond the 'requirements'.

Everyone says hello and goodbye to each other, talks about their weekend, socializes. But this doesn't distract people from making their targets, or learning new things. The most common response to an enquiry is 'I can show you', leading to great information sharing and development of the knowledge and skills of the team members.

These positive interactions – the sharing of knowledge and mutual support – are what lead to an environment of genuine collaboration to achieve the common goal. People personally align to these shared goals – the synergy almost sizzles.

All of these positive interactions between people are what really create the cooperation, energy and team spirit that make a workplace great. And they make life great. However, they can't be 'forced' – they should arise spontaneously. This is where strong trust makes such a difference (and also why it is hard to measure). Strong trust in the manager leads to positive behaviors in the team. It's dynamic, it's cohesive, and it's great synergy.

However, it all starts with you as the manager. So, let's have a look at the benefits for you.

Personal Outcomes

As a manager, you have to work *in* the business: solve problems, provide guidance, and show people things. You have meetings to attend. You also have to contend with your own boss, and therefore, tasks and targets that you have to complete. As a manager, you also have to work *on* the business – to think about where your team is headed and how you are going to get there over the next year or two. This means stepping outside of the day to day 'in the business' to get a more global view.

If you are the manager of that horrible workplace that we considered earlier, your team probably doesn't trust you. There is little chance of cooperation for the common goal – instead it's everyone for themselves, struggling to *look* their best, not *be* their best – competing for your time and attention. Little fights break out constantly, disputes remain unresolved and bitterness builds up, causing a depressing atmosphere that lingers and provokes more complaints. No problem is resolved without your involvement – so you almost never have time to do your own work. There are never enough hours in the day. You're drained. They're drained.

Conversely, if you're the manager of a high trust team, they work well together, they help each other solve problems, they generate ideas for doing things better. They don't have to be chased to achieve their targets; they generate the effort and motivation themselves. For you, the manager, there's plenty of time to plan for the future, to work on the business.

In your high trust environment, people in your team will take the risk to innovate, to build on each other's good ideas. Their initiative and creativity really flourish in an environment where there is open discussion of the risks and rewards, of the implications for others in the team. They know that you, the manager, will provide a reliable safety net if things don't go quite to plan. You and your team are one. The synergy is almost electric. You look good; they look good.

The energy, synergy, innovation of the team, the time to work on the business for you and the atmosphere of a great workplace are all of the ingredients that are generated by strong trust. They are the same ingredients that create outstanding business performance. Now it's time to have a look at what builds strong trust.

Building Trust

What building blocks do you need to build trust? First of all, how are your team members going to judge you? Maybe by how good you are at your own work? Do you have the skills and abilities that are respected in your workplace? Can you do what you are asking other people to do? Were you promoted to manager due to merit? Or, were you promoted into your managerial role as a form of damage control? Can people in your team rely on your professionalism, your ability to handle situations, and to assist them in the actual work to be done? If so, great. But there's more.

Mounting evidence strongly suggests that you can only build outstanding performance when you are *both* professionally good *and of good character*.[4] Professional competence alone is not enough to build an outstanding team. Through your consistent behavior and daily interactions, your team are seeing and experiencing who you really are behind the role. They are sizing you up as a person. Always. And we all do it. Always.

The small things really DO matter.

There is a common expression 'the thing you walk past is the thing you accept'. Similar to having to 'walk the talk', these sayings express the fact that your people make an assessment of your character over time and all the time. You are assessed on your behavior, your consistency and your motivations. You are read like a book as the team builds a picture, based on your reactions – what you react to, when you react and how you react. You might not know that your jaw clenches in a particular way when you're really annoyed. Or you fiddle with your pen, or your phone when you're questioning the actions of a someone. Your team notices. You might be able to trick people into trusting you in the short-term through personal charm, or through 'quick fix' techniques, but in the long-term, people work out who you really are. This is what is meant by *character* – the particular combination of qualities in a person – who they really are behind the projected persona. Who YOU really are.

It takes time for all of us to assess motivations and to observe behavior in different situations. But the good thing about a workplace is that most people are seen at their best, and their worst. Just the constant exposure of people to each other day in day out, week in and week out means that people's veneers are eventually worn away. We see who people really are.

You can trick people into trusting you for a while, even for a long while, but eventually, the true person is revealed.

People have been studying humanity for millennia, so good character has been highly valued for a very long time. Ancient civilizations valued good character and connected it to the virtues. For example, the Greek philosopher Aristotle defined good character as the life of right conduct – right conduct in relation to other persons and in relation to oneself.

Fast forward to more recent times, Dirks and Ferrin's (2002) model shows that the character of the manager affects trust.[5] The character of a manager shapes the attitudes and reactions of employees. Trust and character are strongly related. As we've seen, this makes sense intuitively. But it's helpful to have our intuitions validated. What we think is true is also shown in numbers.

Trust within workplaces relies on the perceived character of managers.[6]

So, character is crucial – especially for managers. However, since about seventy years ago, putting profits before trust has led to quick fixes and personality-based techniques linked to measurable performance outcomes. In other words, adjust behavior to get what you want. Just do it. You don't have to believe it. Recent research, however, contradicts this. It says that you actually have to believe it and what you believe forms your character. This character-based view of humanity dominated up until World War II.[7] After that, the tide changed, and character was downplayed or ignored. Now the tide is reversing, "increasingly educators at colleges and universities are recognizing the importance of educating for that elusive thing called character."[8]

Similarly, in the management literature, there is an important link between character and management competence:

"To educate our character, we must develop habits which strengthen our will and... decision making on a rational basis, integrity, emotional intelligence, and self-control." [9]

What do we mean by character? Good character is widely regarded as having virtues – the repeated good actions that become habits. This means that it is something that we can improve through practice![10] But at the same time, it's not something that we can engineer with a quick fix. Most people realize that character is multi-dimensional. It's too complex to fake, at least consistently. However, you can start by thinking about how you see yourself – what sort of person are you? What sort of person do you want to be?

One commonly used exercise to consider this at a deeper level is to imagine yourself listening to the eulogy at your own funeral. Take some time to ask what sorts of things would you like to hear people saying about your life? What would you like to hear about what motivated you? At the same time, what are the things that you don't want to hear? If you are honest, what will you probably hear? I didn't say this was going to be easy.

You can use your reflection on these questions to adjust your mindset and your sense of self. You can decide to direct your efforts over time into achieving what is important to you – such as leaving a great legacy in the lives of the people in your team and others around you. The great thing is that we all have strengths and weaknesses, and through practice, we can overcome our weaknesses and build on our strengths.[11] It takes time and effort, but if we start in one area and seek to improve in small ways each day, we can reach the end of our life being much happier in ourselves and having helped many people!

To summarize, we have seen that outstanding performance requires trust, and trust requires good character. In the next chapter, we will examine the results from a survey that sought to identify whether aspects of character separate good and bad managers. After summarizing the results of the 1175 responses, we identify the key areas where the best managers excelled. The following chapters then detail how we can apply those lessons to ourselves.

Chapter 3 discusses the first area that we need to consider as managers – learning from mistakes. It is important to approach any improvement effort, realizing that we won't succeed on every occasion. It takes time. Thanks to the research of Dr Carol Dweck and her colleagues, we know we are best placed to approach improvement with a growth mindset. [12]

Chapter 4 looks at the first element of good character – motivation. There is a tension between wanting to 'get ahead' in our own career and helping each team member to be 'the best person they can be'. We look at how the best managers successfully resolve this tension.

Chapter 5 looks at honesty and consistency. Once again, there is a tension between telling the truth and considering the readiness of the person or the team to receive it. Consistency is related to honesty because a person's character is assessed over time. Being consistent in our behavior and our interactions is a key component of building a good character.

Communication is key because it is how we convey a common goal, how we motivate, and how we interact with our team. Chapter 6 considers the ways that the best managers communicate.

Chapter 7 looks at the importance of delegating work. The way that the best managers delegate work helps team members to grow in their capacity and in their careers.

Chapter 8 considers ways we can involve the team in decision making. We discuss how the best managers develop their team by involving them in decisions.

The final chapter looks at how we can be a role model. Many of the best managers were an inspiration to people in their team. People wanted to be like them and looked to them for inspiration. These great managers could motivate people to achieve more and become better through their example, often without realizing it.

Before examining the survey results, take a moment to reflect on the current situation for you and the people you manage. Remember – it doesn't matter where things are now – you can improve things!

To make a start, take just 5 minutes a day for one working week.

Reflect for 5 minutes on Day 1, and then identify one small change for Day 2 based on your reflection.

See an example to try out below.

Start your journey with just 5 minutes a day

Day 1: Reflect on the level of interaction and socialization in your team.

Day 2: Choose one thing from this chapter to try today that would improve on Day 1.

Day 3: Reflect on whether your team members bring ideas to you?

Day 4: Choose one thing from this chapter to try today that would improve on Day 3.

Day 5: Reflect on what you have learned from trying these things. Which positive outcomes could you continue to build on next week?

Chapter 2:

Best and Worst Manager Survey

<u>In this Chapter:</u>

- The mindset and motivation of the best and worst managers
- The behavior of the best and worst managers in communication, honesty and consistency
- The application of these ideas of the best and worst managers in decision making and delegation

https://dominicmcloughlin.com/

Many people have encountered both good and bad managers, but it is difficult to identify the exact numbers in each category. Anecdotally, bad managers seem to be more numerous, partly because people who are good at their role are promoted, but do not receive the appropriate support and training needed to excel at the 'people management' that a managerial role requires. In my experience, this is likely to lead to more of a defensive, 'survival' mentality for these managers. This in turn generates an unhappy workplace, leading to more defensiveness on the part of the manager. As these managers strive to get ahead, they move up the organization with this approach, because they don't know another way. One research report suggests that 18 percent of managers demonstrate a high level of talent for managing others, while another 20 percent have some talent for it.[13] The 62 percent remaining would explain why many people feel that the majority of managers are bad.

In this chapter we are starting with the worst managers, because that is the most common. However, the goal of the book overall is to change the situation by providing simple but effective practical management ideas. These ideas do not require an MBA, but are based on experience and human qualities that we can all understand and identify with. Bad managers are probably stressed managers because they don't feel they have the tools, so they pretend they do.

To test my observations of various forms of management over the years, I undertook a PhD which looked at trust within organizations and more specifically, how the manager's character affected the degree to which he or she was trusted. [14] I surveyed people from several countries about the best manager they ever had, asking them to agree or disagree with a number of character statements about that manager. The same process was applied to the worst manager they had with the same survey questions. The survey yielded over 1175 responses from working people across the US, the UK, Canada, Australia, the Philippines and others. The results were enlightening.

Table 1: Summary of Survey Responses*

	Best Managers	**Worst Managers**	**Difference**
They honored their commitments	87%	12%	**75%**
They followed words with actions	88%	13%	**75%**
They were honest	87%	13%	**74%**
They overcame difficulties	83%	17%	**66%**
They based decisions on the 'right thing to do' rather than 'making money'	75%	11%	**64%**
They put the needs of those reporting to him/her before their own needs	72%	25%	**57%**

*Based on the research in this Chapter

In addition to these results, each person was asked to provide some comments about their best and worst manager. Analyzing the comments for themes[15] and combining them with the results above, the chapters in this book took shape. Four key elements for building team trust are the manager's mindset, motivation behavior and application. The diagram below is a graphical illustration of the relationships.

Figure 1: Character influences trust, which influences performance*

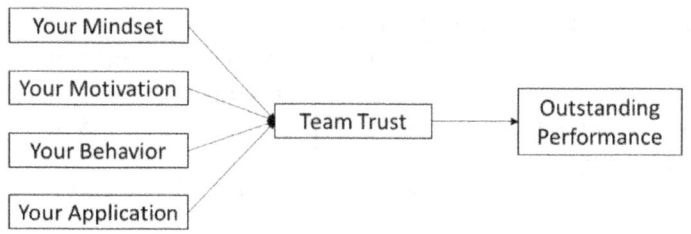

*Based on the research in this Chapter

This analysis also developed a 'sketch' of what the best and worst managers looked like to their team. A brief summary of the attributes of the worst managers is provided here, highlighting the contrasting mindset, motivation and behavior. Practical applications and examples from the best managers are provided in the following chapters.

The Mindset of the Worst Managers

The worst managers refused to take ownership of any poor decisions, bad outcomes or errors. Rather these managers would shift the blame onto team members, leaving them deal with any consequences. Some of the worst managers would choose someone to blame based on race or gender. This resulted in most team members being reluctant to try anything, in case it went wrong.

Two other characteristics of the worst managers – a lack of development opportunities and resistance to change exacerbated this lack of confidence. The worst managers perceived any increase in a team member's skills as a threat to their own position, so they would not provide any positive feedback and would discourage training and development for team members. Similarly, the worst managers were not open to change, such as suggestions to improve processes or the working environment. If a change was enacted and successful anyway, the worst managers would take the credit, leaving those who had done the hard work demotivated and unwilling to innovate in the future.

The Mindset of the Best Managers

In contrast, the best managers were able to foster a learning environment, where team members were not afraid to make mistakes, but focused on learning from them. These managers helped to create this environment by taking responsibility for their own actions, and decisions. Most importantly, the best managers would admit when they had made a mistake, which led people to describe them as 'down to earth' and 'humble'. We will explore this mindset of learning from mistakes in Chapter 3.

The Motivation of the Worst Managers

The worst managers were characterized as 'only caring about themselves'. Their motivation was to benefit themselves above any other concern, creating a good image for their boss. Their goal was to maintain their power and their position, to advance their career and to maximize monetary benefits (usually bonuses). The worst managers would happily make people redundant for a marginal increase in profitability. These attitudes resulted in frustration for the team and a sense of being 'just a number'. They manifested this motivation in unrealistic expectations of the team, with little concern for the needs of individuals or their wellbeing. From the perspective of the team members, these worst managers did not have their best interests at heart, nor even that of the organization. The worst managers had no regard for personal problems. When issues such as sickness, stress or trauma affected someone's the worst managers lacked the capacity and/or the inclination to understand, reacting instead with anger if team members raised such issues.

The worst managers used three principal methods for controlling their teams – 'divide and rule', 'intimidation', and 'micromanagement'. Sometimes they would use all three. The divide and rule method created 'in groups' who would receive good treatment from the manager and 'out groups' who would receive the worst rosters and the most tedious or difficult work. These managers played politics within the team, even intentionally caused conflict among co-workers through gossip, backstabbing and encouraging employees to spy on each other. This caused a serious negative effect on interpersonal relationships and teamwork. Using intimidation to get things done would take the form of threatening people's jobs and even 'blackmailing' them through threats of negative reviews or being blamed for anything that went poorly. Those managers who micromanaged would demand that they approve every decision, no matter how small.

They would use surveillance tools to observe their team at any time and created an atmosphere of looking over everyone's shoulder. These managers were seen as having 'trust issues' and were called 'control freaks'.

Using 'divide and rule', 'intimidation', and 'micromanagement' created a 'harsh' or 'strict' working environment that led to resentment among the team.

The Motivation of the Best Managers

The best managers were distinguished by an ability to strike an appropriate balance between the needs of individuals, the team and the organization. They were often described as 'selfless'. They thought about the needs of team members before their own needs and sometimes sacrificed their own comfort and bonuses, which enhanced employee job satisfaction and performance. This genuine interest in the professional growth of team members created opportunities for learning such as training, coaching and mentoring, which increased the knowledge and skills of the team. We will explore the difference between a motivation centered on self-versus-others in more detail in Chapter 4.

The Behavior of the Worst Managers – Dishonesty and Inconsistency

The worst managers were seen as dishonest, prepared to use deceit to manipulate employees, for example promising a reward that never came, or a promotion that was never available. They often lied about their performance to advance their careers – claiming the work of others as their own and taking all the recognition.

However, if the results were poor, they blamed team members. Some even stole equipment or money from their organization. These managers often had a hidden agenda for the things they did, such as to become more popular. Other forms of dishonesty related to overworking the team and underpaying them. Sometimes this was achieved through failing to hire enough people to manage the amount of work, or not replacing people who left, while maintain the same level of output.

Inconsistency was also seen as a form of dishonesty when there were different rules for different team members. The worst managers treated staff based on the level of friendship. Employees that were liked or 'friends' with the managers came first in getting rewards and roster. Those who were not liked got punished were excluded from meetings and were assigned difficult tasks. Similarly, the worst managers treated people differently, depending on their position in the organization. They were friendly to those in a similar or a higher-level position, but treated subordinates as 'dirt' and spoke to them condescendingly. Employees who were treated this way felt that they were considered 'property' rather than human beings generating a feeling of 'inferiority' and 'powerlessness'. They also manifested inconsistency in the circumstantial application of rules and guidelines based on the manager's opinion at the time, so that there in any given situation there was no certainty for team members of the 'right approach'.

<u>The Behavior of the Best Managers – Honesty and Consistency</u>

As shown in the table above, doing the right thing, rather than the easiest or most profitable, was a highly regarded characteristic of the best managers. Honesty, including following through on commitments, and following words with actions meant that the best managers were considered 'reliable', 'genuine' and 'sincere' which fostered trust between the managers and their team members. We will explore this further in Chapter 5.

The Behavior of the Worst Managers – Communication

The worst managers who did communicate often allowed their emotions to affect how they acted in the workplace. Some were impatient or immature in their approach to team members. Some even humiliated their team members by yelling and shouting at them in front of customers and co-workers. Often this shouting and screaming was for no apparent reason or 'simple matters' that could have been easily resolved. These managers were characterized as 'self-centered' and 'unapproachable'. The worst managers communicated rules and guidelines that were not easily understood, or seemed arbitrary, leaving the team confused. This made it hard to work with them.

Another group of the worst managers avoided communication, 'hiding in their office', unable to deal with the different personalities and approaches in the team. On rare occasions when the team's view was sought, the worst managers disregarded any issues raised, and went ahead anyway. It appeared to be 'all about them' and 'what they wanted'. They acted as if they knew it all and needed no discussion. They also could not resolve any disputes that arose between team members, or between their team and other teams in the organization. All of these behaviors caused these managers to be considered unsupportive and disrespectful.

The Behavior of the Best Managers – Communication

In contrast to the behaviors listed above, the best managers were described as being available for team members to access at any time. In the same way they were described as 'approachable', 'easy to talk to, and 'calm'. When something went wrong, these managers controlled their emotions and maintained good relationships throughout their interactions. They appreciated team members, with good performance being recognized publicly through rewards such as praise, presents, lunches and promotions. At the same time the best managers were open to suggestions, valuing the contributions of all team members. Good communication was reported as building excellent motivation and team morale. We will consider the communication of the best managers further in Chapter 6.

Application of the Worst Managers – Decision Making and Delegation

The worst managers rarely sought feedback or input in making decisions, even when there were detrimental effects on team members. When decisions were not communicated openly, team members felt 'left in the dark'. This lack of transparency by the worst managers was also experienced when they did not take time to explain why decisions were made, leading to unproductive speculation among the team. Some managers even went as far as bullying and intimidating team members into accepting new policies and decisions. Another group of the worst managers were poor at deciding because of inexperience, meaning that no deliberate decision was made. Inaction would then take matters out of their control or inhibit positive changes. A last group would allow discussions about a decision to become so charged with emotional reactions, that no decision could be agreed upon.

Regarding delegation, there were two opposite tendencies – the 'hands off' approach and the 'micromanagement' approach. The worst managers that used the 'hands off' approach delegated all the work and did not assist in any way. They spent no time guiding or assisting in the completion of the tasks. They did not care if the tasks were assigned to the right people, or whether there were enough resources available. A typical response when a lack of resources was pointed out was 'you will just have to work harder'. Team members found this unfair. Those managers who micromanaged would demand that they approve even the smallest decision, meaning that team members had no opportunity to exercise their own initiative. Similarly, the team could not move ahead until they had a decision from the manager, often leading to unnecessary delays. Team members found this 'suffocating' and 'incredibly frustrating'.

<u>Application of the Best Managers – Decision Making and Delegation</u>

In comparison, the best managers made decisions that considered the impact on the business while involving team members in the decision-making process. This approach also involved being transparent, explaining exactly how and why decisions were being made within the organization. The best managers also overcame difficulties by working with individuals (and the team) to find the best solutions for changes that were needed or for customer complaints. Finally, the best managers trusted their team members. They set expectations, provided the necessary resources, and then allowed team members to decide on their own work processes.

The Worst Managers are not Inspiring

Research has shown that managers not only impact on their team members, but on the families of those people as well.[16] In this last section, those responding to the survey pointed out that the worst managers did not lead by example and did not follow through on their commitments. This meant that they did not have the respect of their team. Sometimes the worst managers would use a dictatorial approach and sometimes they clearly valued profit over people. Some of the worst managers did not show any appreciation for the effort put in by team members because nothing was ever good enough. Some were described as having 'big talk but no action' because they would renege on promises, particularly related to incentives and rewards.

The worst managers also cared little about their work and just rushed through it. They did the bare minimum, and at times would give the manager's own responsibilities to team members. Some of the worst managers were seen as incompetent. They were unsuited to the role because of a lack of experience, knowledge, or management skills. These managers were characterized as 'having no clue', 'having no idea what's going on' and this led to team frustration. In the very worst examples, managers went as far as illegal behavior such as engaging in or condoning sexual harassment, accepting bribes from suppliers and stealing ideas or money. The workplace under these managers was described as 'toxic', 'unsafe', and 'destructive'.

The Best Managers are Inspiring

By contrast, the best managers created a workplace that was perceived as 'safe', 'open', 'comfortable', 'fun', 'free of stress', 'engaging', 'clam', 'happy', 'supportive', and promoted learning. They created a low stress work environment that team members enjoyed working in. Inspirational managers were concerned with creating a great customer experience by listening to clients, putting their needs first, and providing an excellent service. Whenever the workload was high, they rolled up their sleeves helped with doing the 'dirty work'. The best managers were very competent. They were described as 'smart', 'intelligent', 'competent', and 'capable'. They had the experience, knowledge, and skills to accomplish the work objectives and had a good understanding of the broader working environment. We will consider these aspects in more detail in Chapter 8.

Figure 2: How Mindset, Motivation and Behavior build Success (based on the research in this Chapter)

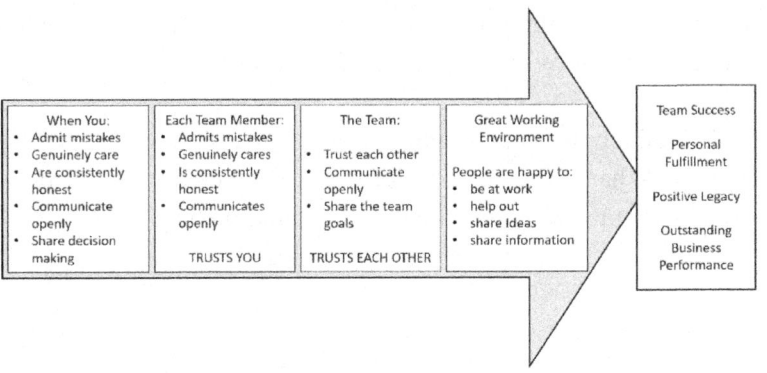

Having given an overview of the characteristics of the worst managers from the survey results, we now turn to examine in more detail how to adopt the mindset, motivation and behavior of the best managers. As illustrated in Figure 2, this is what builds trust and business performance. The survey has revealed what matters most to those responding, and there's a very strong likelihood that they are what matters most to your people too.

Start your journey with just 5 minutes a day

To make a start on your improvement journey, take just 5 minutes a day for one working week. Just reflect for 5 minutes on Day 1, and then identify one small change for Day 2 based on your reflection. See suggestions below:

Day 1: Reflect on your mindset and motivation.

Day 2: Choose one thing from this chapter to try today that would improve on one thing from your Day 1 reflection.

Day 3: Reflect on your honesty and consistency.

Day 4: Choose one thing from this chapter to try today that would improve on one thing from your Day 3 reflection.

Day 5: Reflect on your communicating, decision making and delegation. What have you learned from trying these things? Which positive outcomes could you continue to build on next week?
You can improve things!

Chapter 3:

Mindset – Learning from Mistakes

©dominicmcloughlin.com

In this Chapter:

- Seeing mistakes as opportunities
- Your attitude to mistakes impacts on trust
- Good character

At its core, managing well is about becoming a better person ourselves, and helping those we manage to become the best people that they can be. Even if this has become a cliché, there is truth in it.

This is not about results, or 'doing' things. Rather it is about the journey we are all on as people. Mistakes – and we all make them – are part of any organization. How we as managers deal with them – both our own and those of our team – are often the litmus test that separates good managers from the bad. When things run smoothly and according to plan, managing a team is like overseeing a well-oiled machine. It just needs a drop of oil every now and again. However, if mistakes are made, and things go wrong then it can be a nightmare, despite organization, planning and forecasting. This is where good managers really shine.

As we saw in Chapter 2, the best managers were able to foster a learning environment, where team members were not afraid to make mistakes, but focused on learning from them. These managers helped to create this environment by taking responsibility for their own actions, and decisions. Most importantly, the best managers could admit when they had made a mistake. This led people to describe them as 'down to earth' and 'humble'. So how do we put this into practice?

Mistakes as Opportunities

I'm sure you've heard the saying 'mistakes are learning opportunities'. The theory that any mistake is an opportunity to be curious about ourselves and others is wonderful – until serious mistakes are made. How, when mistakes take their toll and fingers are being pointed, can we develop the mindset that turns this nice theory into practical reality? What do we do, as managers, when mistakes are made? This is where trust pays dividends. Trust is great when things go well. To say where, how, and by whom mistakes were made requires raw honesty. When we make them (and we will), then we are especially under the scrutiny of our team.

If you have made a mistake, what are you going to do? Pretend nothing happened, hope nobody notices so your authority remains intact? Pretend that it wasn't really a mistake, you were just keeping the rest of the team on their toes? Amazingly, supposedly mature adults do actually do this! Shift the blame? Or, do you own up and say 'I was wrong', or 'not the results we were hoping for – let's work through this for a solution?

Owning your own mistakes is a major trust building moment. If you own your mistakes, and other members of your team know it, you are not hiding. You are making yourself *vulnerable* – and how the team reacts to this – says a lot about them as individuals and as a team. If they point the finger and want your blood, you know that you have a lot of work to do in building trust. If they rise to the occasion, and work through things to rectify them, then each of them will feel secure and safe to admit their own mistakes should they arise. And so will you. Because the best managers encouraged learning from mistakes, they also frequently provided feedback on their team's performance, whether it was good or bad. The best managers took A coaching approach, which meant that they were willing to guide employees through challenging job-related tasks. This can only happen if a team member feels able to acknowledge an area of weakness. If you are prepared to be vulnerable, your team will see that it is safe for them to be vulnerable. They will be happy to acknowledge areas where they need development. When they make mistakes, they will own them, and the team can move on.

The fear of inadequacy, or of 'being discovered' (as a fraud) is something that many people have in their secret selves to some degree. In fact, this can be more of an issue for high achievers.[17] Another name for it is 'the imposter syndrome' – we all feel like imposters to some extent, and can live in perpetual fear of being found out.

But if it was all our fault – so what? Some things are only learned by making mistakes. We have learned a valuable lesson which we will be sure not to repeat. We will be a better person and a better manager. Similarly, if the mistake was all the fault of someone in our team, this is a significant moment to help that person grow. Handled well, they can learn a valuable lesson that they will be sure not to repeat and so that person grows and the team becomes stronger.

Finally – and the most likely scenario – is that there were several contributing factors. Through being curious about what caused a mistake, we can get to the bottom of any number of issues – poor communication, poor collaboration, poor processes, poor decision making. If they can be resolved, all of these are vital opportunities for creating long-term success.

However, in the end, it's about trust

All of this sounds straightforward, but it depends on an environment of trust in your team. People are not prepared to reveal a mistake if they don't trust you to help them resolve it. To put it another way, why would you give your boss something to hold over you? Therefore, how we as managers respond to something going wrong, is critical to determining whether anything will be revealed to us in the future. Although the immediate reaction might be to jump up and down, rip out some hair and shout a lot, this is not only counter-productive right now, it will determine whether we ever hear about a problem in the future.

The Qantas Approach

Hearing about problems is critical in the aviation industry–the cost of not correcting them can be disastrous. In the 1990s a Qantas pilot was flying into Hong Kong. With the old airport there wasn't much room for error, as the plane came in to land with massive skyscrapers on either side. The pilot made a simple mistake, reaching above his head and pushing the wrong button. He immediately corrected the error, and no one noticed. To maintain a world class safety record, Qantas had a 'no-blame' policy, so immediately after the safe landing, the pilot reported the error. It turned out that Boeing had moved the button he thought he was pushing and, because he revealed the error, Boeing reverted the buttons back to the position that the pilots were accustomed to. This honesty and vulnerability by the pilot probably prevented someone else making the same error with more drastic consequences.

The Trap

Perhaps the hardest part of establishing this culture of learning from our mistakes, of trust, is the need to lead by example. We, as managers, must be prepared to be more reflective – more aware of what is going on around us, and of our own actions. When we make a mistake, we should be the first ones to apologize and rectify.

We have to be more vulnerable than we are comfortable being.

If we really believe that we, and our team, will grow through openness and honesty, we have to live that – and it's not easy! If our own actions are generally inconsistent, what we say will only be the latest fad or jargon – and people can see through that… just as we can when a CEO, a Board member or a politician does it to us.

Trust is essential, but it does not develop instantly, and it can be easily undermined. There is an old Scandinavian saying that captures this reality very well:

Trust arrives on foot and leaves on horseback!

This is where we can see a key connection between curiosity and trust. Being curious and open to learning about ways that we can improve requires acknowledging that we are not perfect. The world around us is busy saying that success is generated by projecting a perfect image – 'we have to model excellence' – so it can seem strange that being vulnerable in this way can lead to success. However, if we consider the best relationships in our lives, usually they are with people that know us well, including our strengths and our weaknesses. Sharing the fact that we are struggling in some areas is actually a wonderful common ground for building genuine relationships and therefore trust.

Curiosity is important in another sense too, when we are managers. We need to spend a bit more time thinking about the way our words and actions are perceived too. This is because, whether or not we realize it, people are looking at us all the time. People notice the things that we ignore as well as the things that we pay attention to. Curiosity is important because we want to understand the different backgrounds, education, upbringing and experiences of our team. Even the things that we do thoughtfully and intentionally have a certain degree of interpretation by the receiver. Getting to know our team members helps us to better understand the things that are important to them, and how they may interpret the things we say and do.

Let's look at an example

Imagine that you are a new teacher, recently graduated, and your manager (the head of the department) has been teaching for many years. School starts in two weeks. You are trying to organize your classes, but it just isn't coming together like you had hoped – it is a more arduous task than you had imagined. You are not sure how to divide the material; you do not know whether to give homework or have quizzes, or both.

One beautiful Saturday afternoon, your head of department comes over to help you organize your material for the first term. You realize that there are many possible motivations for this generous act. Your manager may be acting out of sympathy for you, or because of the good that will come from it (good classes, good for students and good for their peace of mind).

You appreciate the help that you have received, but it is only over time that you will be able to assess why that manager has helped. Over time, you will be able to assess if the help that was given was truly a selfless act, or whether it is actually part of some scheme to hold something over you or some 'power game'.

Now put yourself into the role of the head of department. You have given up time that you would rather have spent on other things – it is a beautiful day after all. You have done that because you remember what it's like to be new. You remember a great boss that helped you when you first started and how much you appreciated that. You want to ensure that your staff member, the students and the department all improve over time.

The trap that we can fall into as managers is thinking that people should be able to read our motivations. We know that we have that new staff member's best interests at heart – but they don't! It will take the rest of the year for that new staff member to assess what motivates us. They will take time to see by our words and actions whether we are trustworthy, whether we have their back. In other words, the people who work for us have to make an assessment about our character.

A surprising benefit of being open to learning from our mistakes is newfound freedom. We don't have to keep up a façade. We don't have to live in constant fear of something going wrong, of 'looking bad'.

Good Character

The ancient Greek philosopher Aristotle defined *good character* as the life of right conduct – in relation to other persons and in relation to oneself. He made the point that the virtuous life includes self-orientated virtues (such as self-control and moderation) as well as other-orientated virtues (such as generosity and compassion), and the two kinds of virtue are connected.

The best managers not only know the ideas techniques required by their profession. They have developed habits – ways of being – that enable them to apply that knowledge and those techniques successfully: habits of paying attention to others, concentrating on their work, punctuality, coping with success, coping with failure, persevering in their effort, even in difficult times. This is character.

In the next Chapter we will look at a foundational element of good character – our 'self-orientation' and our 'other-orientation'. There is a tension between our motivation for 'getting ahead' in our own careers and wanting to help each team member to be the best person they can be. Before we look at how the best managers resolve this tension, take a moment to reflect on the current situation for you, and the people you manage. Let's try some things and learn from the things that go well AND from anything that doesn't go so well.

Before moving to that chapter, take some time to make a start on your improvement journey, take just 5 minutes a day for one working week. Just reflect for 5 minutes on Day 1, and then identify one small change for Day 2 based on your reflection.

Start your journey with just 5 minutes a day

Day 1: Reflect on your attitude when you make a mistake.

Day 2: Choose one thing from this chapter to try today that would improve on one thing from your Day 1 reflection.

Day 3: Reflect on your attitude when someone else makes a mistake.

Day 4: Choose one thing from this chapter to try today that would improve on one thing from your Day 3 reflection.

Day 5: What have you learned from trying these things? Are there any negative outcomes you can learn from? Which positive outcomes could you continue to build on next week?

Chapter 4:

Motivation – Self and Others

©dominicmcloughlin.com

In this Chapter:

- Self-focused manager versus team-focused manager
- Why bother with the effort?
- Keeping good people
- Building the team

https://dominicmcloughlin.com/

As we saw in Chapters 2 and 3, the best managers 'have your back' in helping you to improve as a professional, and as a person. The survey showed that the best managers could strike an appropriate balance between the needs of individuals, the team and the organization. They showed genuine concern for both individual and team needs which promoted employee commitment and made the workplace less stressful. These managers would advocate for their team members, particularly in the realm of fair compensation for the work they had done. They balanced the need for wellbeing and profit, avoiding 'working people into the ground'.

The best managers were able to empathize with the things that team members were going through in their personal life; sickness, mental health problems, family issues, and understanding how this could affect their performance. They could put themselves into the team member's shoes and assist. This sometimes meant changing established working hours to accommodate these needs.

Similarly, the best managers put team members first, and were often described as 'selfless'. They thought about the needs of team members before their own needs and sometimes sacrificed their own comfort and bonuses. This enhanced employee's job satisfaction and performance. This genuine interest in the professional growth of team members created opportunities for learning such as training, coaching and mentoring which increased the knowledge and skills of the team as a whole.

Being genuinely interested in the team, meant that the best managers encouraged people to work together and even to organize non-work social events. They also helped team members to create professional connections outside of the organization. Friendships often resulted from the genuine care demonstrated to team members, providing encouragement in difficult times, resulting in higher job satisfaction and better performance.

Did you know that good senior managers and good human resources managers keep an eye out for those who help members of their team, as well as working hard themselves? In fact, one key reason why many managers struggle when put into a management position is that the job is no longer 'managing my time and working hard'. "I" am no longer the key element in the equation – now it is about "we" and "us". It is about how well the team does, how well each person in the team contributes and is enabled to contribute.

It's pretty clear that there are many approaches to managing people. However, two underpinning elements influence the thinking. Your *view of yourself*, and your *approach to others*.

In the previous chapter, we considered the importance of being prepared to learn from your mistakes, and being open to others learning from their mistakes. This approach allows for continuous improvement over time and creates an atmosphere of safety. In this environment, your people can seek advice, try new things and grow as a person. It also emphasizes your role as 'one of the team', all working together to achieve a common goal. You view your role as helping the team to achieve outstanding performance together and as individuals. Let's have a closer look at the two different options.

Option One

You have a personal goal of being seen as a great success. You view yourself as the boss – it's who you are.

As the 'heroic' manager you see yourself as the only person who 'knows', the only one who can 'save the day'. You demand respect and deference. You are the boss, the source of all wisdom. You are entirely focused on your career, your next promotion. The team is there to make you look good. This focus on 'looking good' is vital to your sense of self – although inside you are often terrified of mistakes that will make you look bad. You expect to be moving onward and upward soon, so there is no reason to invest in the people who will be 'left behind'.

An example

Sean was becoming very stressed over a tricky IT project. He knew he was out of his depth. The transition from three customer databases to a new, single database seemed to have a lot more complications than they had led him to believe. Kath was one of the database administrators working for Sean and she was concerned at a number of shortcuts that were being taken to try and finish the project on time. When she pointed out the risks of customer information being mismatched, Sean's response was 'just do it – we're already running a month behind'. Sean happily accepted his manager's praise when he got the project back on schedule. However, those in Sean's team were hassled to put in longer and longer hours, to get things done on time. Sean was always late to the key meetings, unless his manager was attending. He was seen as 'off politicking' rather than helping with the work, which was very demotivating to the team. The obvious risks of things going wrong, and a lack of clear direction, meant that the team members were constantly bickering, seeking to avoid any blame for the inevitable errors that happen when people are both tired and under pressure.

After the latest trial integration failed spectacularly, Kath sought a private meeting with Sean. After outlining the reasons for the latest failure, she suggested that Sean speak to his manager and ask for more time. Kath suggested that the complications that had been identified, the risk of mismatched data and the potential customer inconvenience were good reasons for seeking more time. However, Sean was angling for a good short-term outcome because he was in line for a bonus if they achieved it. Instead of following Kath's suggestion, Sean told his manager that the team members were incompetent, singling out Kath as 'obstructive'. He got agreement to bring in a contractor to 'fix the problems'. In the three months that followed, Kath and about a quarter of the team found jobs with other organizations. Once the project was completed, Sean took all the credit and got his bonus. He immediately left to join the contractor's business. A few weeks after Sean left, it became apparent that the integration had 'left out' some key systems, meaning that the project was not complete at all.

This example highlights the potential dangers when the manager's goal is about their personal success, rather than a goal that benefits team members and the organization. The team was able to assess Sean's underlying goal – as a manager and as a person. We know actions speak louder than words, and that managing people means a manager is under more observation than perhaps they think. Good people left because they were not supported, and were in fact blamed, by their manager.

The other option

You have a personal goal of leaving a great legacy in the lives of your people (and others around you). You view yourself as enabling the team – it's who you are.

This motivation, like all motivations, begins with your perspective and your thinking, and is ultimately reflected in your actions. You provide ongoing help; you guide team members as issues arise; you make time to catch up one-on-one; you coach your people. This shows that you really care and want them to succeed. You are happy to go the extra mile, rather than merely doing the bare minimum. You are available. All of this is reflected in the things that you do for the team in practical ways. You help when things are really busy; you encourage your people to have work life balance, perhaps allowing people to go home early or come in late after a grueling project or week. You really care about the wellbeing of each team member. You take the time to show your appreciation for work that is done well – sometimes one to one, sometimes publicly. You celebrate success.

But the key motivation to the success of all these endeavors is your personal mission. You seek the common goal of the team, the good of the team. You do not put your own good ahead of the group. You contribute your best efforts to the team. You are happy to hear the perspective of others, with sometimes being wrong, with improving over time, so your team see that you are genuine, that this is part of who you are.

https://dominicmcloughlin.com/

This option has a potential disadvantage. It is not possible to see yourself as a friend. You are still responsible for what the team does. You still have to make the decisions.

Example

An inexperienced team, all fairly new to the organization were asked to work on an important project. They were given an experienced manager named John, as the project lead. John saw this as an opportunity to develop each person in the art of project management. In addition, John wanted to find at least one person who could lead such projects in the future.

John led by example, even in seemingly insignificant things. Because he saw the team's time as valuable, he demonstrated it by being in the room at the scheduled start time and began every meeting on time and finished on time. In the first meeting, John asked for everyone's ideas about how best to approach the project. He sought a list of the potential obstacles and estimates of the time that each part of the project would take. It would have been quicker (for John) to just hand out a project schedule and assign people to the tasks at random. Instead, he spoke to each person about which parts of the project were more interesting to them. He checked on each person's previous experience with similar work and asked which areas they wanted to develop their skills in.

As a result of taking some extra time initially, John was able to allocate work that people were genuinely interested in. He had to provide some coaching to those who were challenging themselves in a less familiar area. He did have to sort through some personality clashes and minor issues. He had to correct some people about their interactions with others in the team. However, because they trusted that John had their long-term interests at heart, correction was usually taken well, even if it wasn't immediately welcome. The team became genuinely enthusiastic about the project. As a result, the teamwork around the project developed a synergy that meant that the result was greater than any one particular contribution – finishing on time and to a very high standard. In addition, John was able to find two members of the team that could run such a project themselves in the future. Everyone on the team appreciated the opportunity to understand project management and to improve their skills, their professionalism and their career prospects.

That is why achieving the high levels of trust that leads to outstanding performance (discussed in Chapter 1), you must really become that person – not just learn techniques or 'tricks of the trade'. Eventually your true motivation and true self are revealed.

Why bother?

All of this sounds like a lot of work. Being conscious of what others perceive about my motivations can be tiring. Being vulnerable with my team seems risky. Learning from my mistakes can be embarrassing. Helping team members to grow requires effort. Is it worth it?

The benefits of putting in place these building blocks of trust do deliver fantastic benefits. When your team trust you, they feel that they can point out problems or difficulties. This allows you to have an excellent sense of what is really happening; blockages can be identified and resources to be allocated where they are really needed. By contrast, delays in identifying these problems lead to inefficiency, time and cost overruns.

Where your team trust that you have their best interests at heart, they feel they can express concerns about their own capacity to do a task or project. This in turn allows you to provide what they need for success – whether that is guidance/mentoring, supplementary training or even additional resources. It is only in a work environment of strong trust that people feel safe to say that they need help, and this helps to ensure outstanding performance.

Similarly, you demonstrate that it is okay to ask for help when you don't think that you have all the answers. You are prepared to be vulnerable with your team, so you can go to your team with a problem and genuinely seek their help.

At the same time, you are able to get many different perspectives on the problem and generate more robust solutions through people building on each other's ideas.

Your people feel supported enough to be creative, to spend time thinking about innovative solutions and feel safe enough to put them forward. This is where outstanding performance is generated. Similarly, the loyalty that people feel toward the team, and toward you, means that they are willing to put in the extra work in those difficult times. Your people will 'have your back', because they know that you have theirs.

The alternative is an environment of low trust, where people spend a lot of time and energy crafting their excuses, competing for resources, blaming others and hoarding knowledge to ensure their own survival. All of this time and energy could be directed to the common goal of your team. The loyalty (that we just discussed) is absent in a low trust environment. When times get tough, you look for support, but find that it isn't there – in fact, your people will happily blame you to save themselves.

Keeping Good People

I'm sure you have heard the saying "people don't leave their job – they leave their boss." I wonder how much corporate memory and experience has been thrown away by managers not knowing how to manage. Experience in a particular work environment – knowing who to call, how to sidestep organizational hurdles, how to get the job done is different in every workplace. It requires experience in that workplace. Let's look at some examples of people leaving – with different outcomes.

Hidden Consequences

Linzie had been working as an administrator for a large charity for 10 years. A new manager decided that she was overpaid and they would be better off using a virtual assistant to cut costs. The 'cost saving restructure' went ahead and Linzie was made redundant. It was with a mixture of regret and satisfaction that Linzie heard of the chaos that slowly unfolded across the next 6 months. Thanks to her years of experience Linzie was great at multi-tasking and knew everyone who came into the head office. The virtual assistant could not provide this personal touch and was also way out of her depth because of the complicated way that things had been set up historically.

Almost every day there were comments from clients and donors such as "Where's Linzie, I used to enjoy my chats with her." As the time for new annual donations and tax receipts drew closer, several people approached the manager with things like "I haven't seen the documentation we're waiting on – I used to ring Linzie and she would send it over straight away." The donations that were lost that year were at least double the 'savings'.[18]

Good Departures

Helen had spent several years building up her team. They really believed in the mission of helping those who were less well off. Her tightly knit team over the years had won many awards for going above and beyond their duties to help clients who really needed it. People seldom left her team because it was such a great place to work, and the team grew in size over time. Occasionally, someone who seemed to have the dedication needed at interview, turned out to be not so good. One such person seemed great, but turned out to be quite toxic to the team culture. She was careful not to be too obvious, but over the course of the first 4 months there was too much gossiping about co-workers and too many examples of not doing their fair share of the work, passing tricky cases onto others in the team, always with some excuse. Helen was approached by a number of her long- term team members on different occasions, concerned that the team dynamic was being seriously disrupted. Helen decided she had better discuss the situation before the probationary period ran out.

Although Helen did not like conflict, for the good of the team, she met with the new team member. It was not an easy conversation, but Helen stuck to the facts. She went through her duties in detail, reiterating the importance of professionalism and helping the team. She outlined the success of the team in helping clients over many years. She also provided a clear indication of acceptable and unacceptable behaviors in her team. Helen increased her own monitoring – collecting examples of poor behavior and taking additional time (that she didn't really have) to raise the examples one-on-one with the difficult team member. When the new employee moved on to another organization, the benefits of Helen's approach became apparent. The existing team felt that the positive culture had been preserved. The team trusted Helen to defend the team from poor behavior. Helen had reinforced the standards that she had spent so much time and effort developing.[19]

Building the Team

Strong trust in a workplace also allows for everyone to grow their capabilities and skills, allowing them to take more responsibility. Most people want to do a good job and when you know your people well, you have a good sense of their existing skills, and where they would like to head to in the future. This knowledge of your team's skills, capacities and ambitions, allows you to provide the opportunity for them to step up and try taking a bit more responsibility. They are happy to do so, because they know that you are supporting them. They know that if they make a mistake, you will help them to deal with, and learn from it. This leads to a sustained lifting of your team's capacity and capability. Over time, each team member is better able to deliver on their own role, and to support the team in delivering outstanding performance.

Delegating then becomes easier as your people grow, allowing you as a manager to spend more time thinking about the more strategic issues, or to engage with stakeholders and customers. All of this in turn leads to better job satisfaction, lower turnover, better career prospects and happiness to put in extra effort. In fact, when your people trust you, they will be prepared to share what's going on in their life outside of work – their sports, beliefs, family and friends and you can share yours with them. This creates an atmosphere where people can support each other in all sorts of ways – not just work related.

Here are a couple of examples of how the difference plays out in real life – the first from a school and the second from an accounts department.

Example: Working in a School (in a bad environment)

Whenever Jasmine mentioned her job, she always said that working with high school kids was stressful but also rewarding. She told me that if it hadn't been for her manager and his selfish attitude, then she might've stayed in that job forever, or at least for as long as she could. Alas, it simply wasn't to be, and her Principal Alexander was one of the key reasons why the experience left such a sour taste in her mouth.

Jasmine told me that her classes kept getting a higher proportion of students with learning difficulties year after year, while other classes seemed to not have as many. Besides making her class results seem poor, Jasmine felt that she couldn't allocate enough time to her better students, which was unfair to them. If Alexander had stepped in to properly mix all the classes, or even apply for a teacher's aide, then all of the students could have benefitted from a better learning environment.

But this didn't happen. Alexander was obsessed with a few key aspects of his job. Jasmine and the other teachers didn't seem to be one of these. He ignored their input, their ideas and – finally – their complaints. Instead, he was focused on coming up with 'innovative' educational ideas and plastering them all over the media and internet.

By the time Jasmine had the chance to step up into a more senior role, she couldn't cope with being silenced any longer, especially not when the kids were also suffering because of Alexander's ego. She moved to a better school.

Example: Working in Accounts (in a good environment)

Lorenzo told me he would occasionally spend a moment thinking about a manager he once had in accounts payable. Although he had long since left that job, he still thought about what a superb manager Ricardo had been. Ricardo was in charge of a close-knit team who enjoyed working alongside each other and there was a great atmosphere – except for 'month end' when tensions ran high because of deadlines outside of the team's control. But even then, the team pulled together to deliver. Everyone felt they were in it together.

A shift in management led to higher expectations from everybody, and a reshuffle of normal quotas and deadlines. This meant that Lorenzo and his colleagues had to work harder and longer to get through all of their work on time. Tensions ran high, then went even higher. Everyone got a little more 'on edge' every day, and it got worse and worse.

Ricardo noticed and felt that it was his job, as their manager, to do something about it. Instead of 'cracking the whip', Ricardo went and demanded some answers from the senior management team. Lorenzo found out later that Ricardo had put everything on the line – his seniority, respect, and his position – to improve the situation for his overworked team. It worked. They delegated some responsibilities to another team, and they moved the deadlines to times that were less busy. Once Lorenzo became a manager himself, he always remembered the importance of sticking up for his team, even at risk to his own job.

Conclusions

These examples help to illustrate the difference that managers make. We have seen that the motivation of a manager has many important implications for the performance of the team, the lives of those working in it and for the manager. Enabling the team, being genuinely concerned about the people in your team does deliver outstanding performance. Your motivation, your view of yourself, and your approach to others will ultimately be your management practice. It is rewarding when we see the good fruits of our investment. In fact, we become more motivated to lead our people well.

Reflection on your Motivation

For this reflection, remember that it's not really one or the other. We can think of our focus being more like a scale.

Focus on Self   Focus on the Team

You can use the reflection questions to see where your focus is and where you would like it to be. You can also repeat the exercise considering it from different perspectives:

- Motivation
- Behavior
- Thoughts

To make a start on your improvement journey, take just 5 minutes a day for one working week. Just reflect for 5 minutes on Day 1, and then identify one small change for Day 2 based on your reflection. See the exercise below.

Start your journey with just 5 minutes a day

Day 1: Reflect on your motivation. Are you trying to improve each member of your team?

Day 2: Choose one thing from this chapter to try today that would improve on one thing from your Day 1 reflection.

Day 3: Reflect on whether you see your success and your team's success as the same thing?

Day 4: Choose one thing from this chapter to try today that would improve on one thing from your Day 3 reflection.

Day 5: What steps should you start to take to move along the scale – to being more focused on my team? What have you learned from trying these things?

Are there any negative outcomes you can learn from? Which positive outcomes could you continue to build on next week?

Chapter 5:

Behavior – Honesty and Consistency

©dominicmcloughlin.com

In this Chapter:

- Honesty in the workplace
- Consistency as a part of honesty
- The benefits of honesty and consistency
- Awareness of the impact of perceptions

In the last few chapters, we have seen the importance of generating trust to achieve outstanding performance in a team. Since you've just been appointed as a manager, I would imagine you're there because of your professional and technical expertise. Do you think this is enough? Many poor managers do – to their cost. As a manager, your focus shifts, abruptly. Now you are focused on the team and its goals. For many, this is not an easy shift. Workplaces are littered with people who fail to realize this. Many dysfunctional teams and unhappy team members and toxic workplaces are the result. Good managers have a set of good managerial skills. If you don't know what they are, this chapter is for you. As we saw in Chapter 1, you as the manager set the tone for the team and through your consistent behavior and daily interactions you build the impression that your team has of you over time. We identified some key advantages of an environment where people see us acknowledging our errors and empowering them to do the same. Then, in Chapter 4, we looked at the importance of motivation – establishing how important it is that we are concerned for the good of the team and achieving the team goals.

In this chapter we will look more closely at the honesty and consistency and see how fundamental they are in managing a team. Good managers are honest. We know this because they are truthful, and they are sincere. Most people can have bursts of honesty – but to be genuinely honest means that you are so consistently. We also think of an honest manager as being free of deceit, so we will touch on motivation (as part of honesty) later in this chapter. The survey participants identified honest managers of people who told the truth – not a big surprise.

The key characteristic of the best managers was honesty, with 87% (1022) of the survey participants saying that their best manager was honest. On the other hand, only 13% (152) of the worst managers were seen as honest. This amounts to one of the largest differences in the survey – a 74% difference between the best and worst managers. The numbers attest to the priority that people put on managers being honest. But is that all we need? Let's see.

Closely connected to honesty, but not just being truthful, is the idea of consistency. This adds a certain dynamism to being honest and truthful. Keeping your word or making things true are elements of following through on commitments. This reflects the idea that honesty and truthfulness are a way of operating, and can be thought of as more of a style than just a static personal characteristic. Thinking about the best managers, 87% (1022) of the survey participants said that they honored their commitments, while 88% (1034) said their best manager followed their words with actions. Bad managers were found to follow their words by actions by only 13% (152) of survey participants; only 12% (141) honored their commitments. This second point is the largest difference in the survey – a 75% difference showing how important consistency is as a manager.[20]

Fortunately, much of this is within your control! Honest and consistent people are more considered, more deliberate in building their reputation for honesty and consistency with their team. Let's unpack some of the practical implications of these findings for you as a manager.

Giving Credit

Survey participants identified that strong relationships (generated by honesty and consistency) meant that team members were loyal and happy to work hard. The best managers were prepared to let their people shine, they were not interested in claiming the hard work of others as their own. As we saw in the previous chapter, your concern for the team allows you to report on success by appropriately giving credit to the team. This too has a connection to honesty, because if you take the credit for the work of others, you are not really being honest. How often do you think this happens in the workplace? Too often. The best managers recognized their role in facilitating the success of the team. They like to hide and disappear in the success of the team. Let's have a look at an example.

An Example

Trevor had been asked to design a new layout for the production process, using 3D printers wherever possible to save time and costs. Because it involved the provision of costs for the machines and a new production flow, it was quite a complex task. Trevor wasn't very familiar with the new technology and his initial attempt was 'not good enough' according to his manager. Trevor decided to give one of his team the problem, and Rob was the 'lucky guy'.

Rob spent a lot of time and effort putting together the new proposal, including the various advantages and disadvantages of different 3D printers, providing two alternative production layouts with full costings for each. Rob was secretly hoping that this might be the thing which gained him a promotion, or at least a pay rise. Trevor's rang his manager and said that he had found the solution, not mentioning Rob at all. Trevor's manager was very happy with the work and selected one of the options for implementation.

The message sent to Rob in this incident was that Trevor did not care about Rob's career – he was only interested in furthering his own. Needless to say, this did not inspire Rob to put in his best effort for future projects. Not only that, word quickly spread that Trevor would only use other's ideas and your work to make himself look good. Ideas were seldom shared with Trevor after that.

In this way, we can see that honesty often involves treating others with the respect due to them. In many ways, being honest is not just about speaking the truth, there is a deeper element – often called integrity. Trying to give people their due is part of that. Recognizing the contributions that the team makes to the successes that a manager can report on. As we saw in chapter one, this requires good character – the qualities in you – who you really are. And because it is part of who you are, you behave that way consistently over time.

As an honest manager, you personally care about the truth in what you are telling others.

Your consistency is also relevant because you care about being able to keep your word, to deliver on your commitments. Over time, that leads to an extremely valuable reputation for being reliable, being a 'person of integrity'.

Owning Mistakes

We have already begun this process, because (in Chapter 3) we talked about being vulnerable, being open to learning from our mistakes, and trying to improve. Being humble in this way is to seek the truth about ourselves – knowing both our strengths and our weaknesses. Have you ever noticed that honest people generally have much less fear of making mistakes? Maybe they have nothing to hide. People who know themselves well, also tend to be very understanding towards other people. And the universal truth that everybody makes mistakes is just business as usual for the person who knows themself.

Better understanding of the truth about ourselves allows us to better understand the truth in what we see around us.

Because relationships are so important to us, we are very attuned to honesty and dishonesty – we can smell it. Dishonesty can be tangibly repulsive – whereas, there is something inherently attractive in someone who is honest. Honest people tend to be more calm, more measured in what they say. Honesty tends to be more 'short answers and following through', whereas dishonesty tends to be more 'complicated answers and little or no follow through'.

Resolving Conflicts

Conflicts in the workplace have become more frequent. Difficult situations can arise with little opportunity to prepare, meaning that it is too late to try and generate trust. But if you already have a reputation for being honest and trustworthy, you are much more likely to be trusted by the disputing parties and therefore better able to facilitate dialogue.

Example: Honesty Shines Through

Julie was in a meeting between the national union leader and a national retail manager (and their staff). This union leader had a reputation for honesty and consistency that had been built up over 20 years. As a union leader, he often had to rely on his reputation to resolve disputes and solve problems. Someone once said that his handshake was more valuable than a written contract.

This meeting had been called because for over 2 years a store manager had been operating by giving all the good shifts to the 'in-group' (her friends) and all the worst shifts to the 'out-group'. Despite attempts to get her to change this behavior and allocate shifts fairly, the manager responded by making life for the 'out-group' even harder – reducing hours and scheduling them on the weekends. For some, this meant a big impact on their families.

Eventually, 80% of the staff in that store walked out in protest for half an hour (3pm-3.30pm) – leaving the busy store full of customers with only the manager and her supporters to deal with the customers. This is a very unusual event in the retail industry and had resulted in the company taking notice at the highest levels. The tension across the negotiating table was palpable.

The company began by protesting that they had not been properly informed of the issues faced by the staff (as was required) and that the union members were therefore wrong to organize the walkout. The union replied that the regional manager had been contacted on a number of occasions. In front of his boss (the national manager) the regional manager said 'I have not been contacted'. The union staff member pulled out her notebook and gave four dates when she had called the regional manager – even giving the times.

The regional manager – caught out – appealed to the national union leader: "You're a very busy person, do you return every call you get?"

The union leader only had to say one word. "Yes."

Silence followed. Everyone knew he meant it.

It wasn't clear to Julie at the time why everyone believed it, but in essence *an honest person with a reputation for honesty only has to say one word.* The regional manager was sidelined for the rest of the discussion, with the national manager taking over. The dispute was resolved to the satisfaction of the staff.

Other Benefits of Honesty and Consistency

You have probably seen some of the many books, articles and blogs[21] that point to the importance of keeping your word in business and showing how honesty is important to trust. This is often discussed as important for clients, customers and an organization's public reputation. However, there seems to be less emphasis on how important honesty and consistency is with people inside your organization too. If we treat each other poorly, what about our clients?

Your Team are Honest with You

Where your team members feel that they are in a working environment of safe workplace relationships, there is much less motivation for team members to lie to you.[22] If people feel that they are safe being themselves, they don't have to be constantly proving themselves, they don't have to 'protect their back', so there is less reason to lie.[23]

In essence, your honesty and consistency mean that you will receive more honesty from your team.

Because you are consistent in your actions and reactions, your team are confident that they can come to you for help. Because you always do what you say you will do, there is no reason to fear that you will not follow through. Even the basis for your statements have been taken seriously. Because you hold yourself to account for delivering on your promises, you are also careful to understand the issues thoroughly.

You are Clear-Minded

The honest person can be more clear-minded because they don't have to keep track of what lie has been told to whom. They have more capacity to 'be present' in conversations because they are not having to 'second guess' themselves continually.

One example illustrates this point. A sales manager had an excellent reputation for winning contracts. However, he came undone when someone accidentally phoned the wrong number and left a message demanding payment for his 'commission'. It turned out that the sales manager had been paying kickbacks to the procurement managers whenever a contract was given to him. This one wrong number unraveled a whole web of deceit that led to the sales manager losing his job and facing criminal charges. It had become almost a full-time job trying to manage all the lies, all the contacts and even the false invoices. Everything came apart when the scheme got too big.

In a similar example, Addison was falsifying the accounts, and using the company credit card to buy expensive personal items, and taking work laptops and giving them to friends. Where is Addison's mental energy being engaged? In managing? Yes, managing a web of deceit. Never being able to relax, but always testing the waters – do they know? Am I safe? She looked at me suspiciously – I'd better follow her up to make sure she suspects nothing. How much effort would it require hiding these things over a year, (or five years!). When people lie frequently, they are almost always scanning their environment for fear of being discovered, their minds are whirring to try and keep track of all the different versions that they have told to different people. They fear any mistakes they have made because it could lead to the discovery of the entire deception.

Lies and deception will usually come to light eventually but, however long it is, think of the damage to the morale of a team. The team is suffering from not having the resources that the organization allocated for them. They are using slow out-of-date laptops, because the new ones have been stolen. The budget they should have for training, for travel, for accommodation, and for clients has been greatly reduced due to abuse of the credit card. They are under unrealistic pressure to reduce costs and increase sales, because of the falsifying of the accounts. This is a horrible place to work. They are bleeding from within – and are powerless to do anything about it.

As we have done in previous chapters, imagine how difficult it is to be in a workplace where your manager takes credit for your work, or says that they are going to do something and doesn't do it. When a manager is not concerned for honesty in communication, they will tend to say what they want others to believe, in order to achieve their personal goal. They are often unconcerned about having to fulfill what they say. Imagine the confusion this causes.

What about when they don't pay you correctly or where only their 'friends' get accurate information. Imagine the demotivation and the team members fighting among themselves. Imagine how little that team would get done, and how quickly people would try to leave. These are the genuine possibilities when a manager is not concerned about integrity, about honesty and consistency.

Unfortunately, this is far too common.

Perceptions of Dishonesty

Understanding the disadvantages of dishonesty and inconsistency can help you to be more aware of what you are saying to people. Don't become paranoid – but do remember this when you are making commitments – do not promise something that you will be unable to deliver. Ensure that you take careful note of the undertakings that you make and follow through.

If you say you are going to do something, and don't do it, then it may be perceived as a lie.

Don't be afraid to say 'I'll have a think about that and get back to you'. Similarly, be clear about exactly what you are undertaking to do, trying to avoid gray areas. Finally, in line with learning from mistakes, you need to be prepared to tell someone when you are going to be late in delivering something, or that you have encountered an unexpected hurdle, or when you have been over-ruled.

Although these may seem like hard conversations to have (perhaps you feel like you have failed) the person will find out, eventually. Delaying that inevitable conversation, can make you look unreliable or inconsistent. Genuinely trying to fulfill your undertakings, the reputation you gain for honesty and reliability is worth a lot.

A Test of Honesty

An assessment of someone's honesty is so key to personal relationships that people are often attuned to signs of dishonesty. Think, for example, about your reaction when someone tells you how honest they are. This has important implications for us as managers.

A simple example might be when someone says "Who left that dirty cup in the lunch room? We're supposed to wash our own things." It happens everywhere. People assume someone will do it. If it was you, it is a chance to own up to it. This is a very small thing, but if it was you, and someone knows, you can be sure that everyone will know by the end of the week. In addition, more and more dirty cups will end up being left unwashed, because that is the example you set by your action/inaction. That is why it is so important that honesty is part of who you are, part of your character. That way these little tests are another opportunity to enhance your reputation for honesty and consistency.

A Test of Integrity

Let's look at a common destructive element – gossip. Jayden is talking to a couple of people in the lunch room. "I know you're worried about the restructure, but don't worry, I heard that Brett is gone. I think it's because he's always coming back from lunch a 'little bit unsteady'. I heard he got done for drink driving recently too."

If you, as the manager of this team, happen to be in the lunch room, your reaction will be noted. For mild gossip, generally a person with integrity will neither engage with the gossip nor condemn the narrator of it, but instead move onto another topic. If it is seriously malicious or destructive gossip (such as in this example) a person of integrity is likely to say something like "Well we don't really know the facts, so we shouldn't be discussing it." [24]

These little tests can occur with no one deliberately 'setting out to test you', but they end up making a difference to how you are perceived by your team. Everyone notices.

A Test of Standards

Similarly, honesty and consistency are very important when there is poor performance. If you accept poor work or poor behavior – that is what you will eventually get from everybody. When you see poor behavior (or poor performance) you need to articulate what needs to change and follow up on it. Most people genuinely want to improve at their job and will respond to constructive feedback.

Even if a person does not want to improve, then you still have to give them that opportunity and make clear that they will not continue to be part of the team if they do not improve. If you ignore poor performance, you are also being unfair to other team members, because that slack has to be picked up somewhere. Those team members who are doing their best will wonder why they bother, when others do not.

You can see from these practical examples of things that arise in the workplace that the way we communicate with our team is a very important element of managing. We will therefore move onto communication in the next chapter. Before doing that, consider your current situation through the exercise below.

Start your journey with just 5 minutes a day

Day 1: Reflect on your honesty with your team.

Day 2: Choose one thing from this chapter to try today that would improve on one thing from your Day 1 reflection.

Day 3: Reflect on your consistency with your team.

Day 4: Choose one thing from this chapter to try today that would improve on one thing from your Day 3 reflection.

Day 5: Reflect on whether you need to have any difficult one-on-one conversation with anyone who is behaving or performing poorly? What can you do next week?

Chapter 6:

Behavior – Communication

©dominicmcloughlin.com

<u>In this Chapter:</u>

- Trust and communication
- Listening in a genuine way
- Developing people through mentoring and feedback
- Giving negative feedback
- Communicating the larger picture
- Virtual communication

In the first few chapters, we have looked at trust, we've looked at mindset and motivation in building trust. We've looked at honesty and consistency. Now, let's look at how these are all shown – their 'face' if you will. How do you communicate?

We know good managers are excellent communicators. Their communication is clear, open, upfront, honest and easily understood. However, there are many different elements to good communication. In the previous chapter, we touched on some practical examples to illustrate the importance of communication. Specifically, being genuinely concerned for truth in your communication to others and dealing with poor behavior (or poor performance) by communicating what needs to change, and following up on it.

Your best manager probably made you feel able to approach them about anything that concerned you. They were available. Similarly, they are likely to have been a mentor for you – helping you to grow both professionally and personally. People responding to the survey said that the best managers they ever had, were caring, open to employee suggestions and developed their employees.

Good communication is based on good relationships. Although techniques can be helpful, it is more important to build your professional relationship with each team member one-on-one. Understanding where each person is in their career, what inspires them and what frustrates them, what they are looking for, their background and preferred communication style are all part of improving your communication with them.

Although communicating with your team as a group is important, people have distinct personalities, backgrounds, experience and learning styles, and would probably prefer to be understood and managed as individuals. It is by having frequent conversations and getting to know people, that the various preferred styles become apparent. This requires you to be proactive – seeking interactions, creating opportunities and building positive working relationships.

One reason for making the effort to build your communication has been highlighted by the pandemic. Many of us have seen into the lives of others through virtual meetings. This has led to many of us being more aware of the external factors that can affect our teams. Seeing a two-year-old running through the room or having a meeting canceled because someone got Covid provide glimpses into the reality that we all have a lot going on in our lives, in addition to our work. As a manager, we want to have a good of understanding of the pressure people may be under outside of work, so that we can offer support and flexibility when it is needed.

Another reason for taking the initiative, seeking interaction, is that your team may not feel that it is appropriate to approach you, unless there is a serious problem. You don't know what experiences they have had in the past. Perhaps they had a manager 'who did not want to be disturbed' – ever! In the survey, people said their worst managers were self-interested, demeaning, lacking in empathy and lazy. So, it is important to show that you are not one of those managers!

By frequently chatting to people in a natural way, your team are more comfortable approaching you about minor issues, and even about their own hopes and needs. It will take time to establish an environment of open communication, but good interpersonal communication directly builds trust.[25] This has always been challenging because managers are time poor, but there are two recent trends which have made it more difficult.

The first trend is the increasing frequency and extent of workplace change.[26] This is leading to more people feeling overwhelmed and fatigued.[27] One 2020 study found that work is entering the biggest era of transformation in decades and that the accelerated pace of business and technology change will continue to put pressure on leaders, showing that nearly 60% of leaders reported they feel used up at the end of the workday – a strong indicator of burnout.[28]

The second trend is the increase of flexible and virtual working. The same 2020 study found that 23% of leaders say they "aren't effective at all at leading virtual teams." Of all the skills surveyed, leaders reported having the least confidence in their digital acumen and ability to lead virtually. [29] While there are undeniable benefits of virtual working, it can also increase the sense of isolation – there are no longer as many opportunities for a casual conversation. Having to 'book a time' to speak, already increases the formality of interactions. Similarly, you can't just put your head over the cubicle and ask a quick question. Communication can seem more distant and formal when it is virtual. It is also difficult to replicate casual workplace interactions that often help to build trust. Interestingly, studies often suggest that trust and team cohesion are remedies to the problem of virtual distance. In this sense, good communication builds trust, and more trust builds better communication.

In this chapter we will consider several aspects of good communication. This is the basis for you to be more thoughtful about how, when and why you communicate. We will consider communication in person and then cover how these same principles may be applied in the digital realm in the last section.

Trust and Communication

One of the significant benefits is that setting a tone of open communication helps all team members to be more open with each other. This in turn facilitates cooperation and creates trust between people and the strong team spirit that creates a great working environment.

An Example

Kira had come from a very difficult workplace. Michael, her previous manager, was a big believer in workplace politics. He analyzed everything that happened as a 'win or loss' for his own power and influence. Kira had been burned the first few times she revealed information to Michael, only to have it used against her in the following weeks. As a result, Kira had adapted to survive the environment by using similar techniques.

When she moved to a new organization, she set about building a power base, as she had seen Michael do. Kira spent the first few weeks getting to know the people she was working with – getting them to understand how lucky they were to have her to identify all the problems in the new organization. Because of the support she generated, and the problems identified, Kira was able to bring in some of her former staff across to the new organization to solve those problems. Within three months she was in charge of a third of the organization and had five former staff working for her.

When Angelo took over as General Manager, he wanted to build an environment of trust, strong team spirit and cooperation. He began by having one-on-one meetings with every staff member and slowly built a map of how the organization worked. As part of his investigation and observation, Angelo uncovered a few elements that he found concerning. The first was the amount of distrust of Kira and her 'team'. There were many independent stories of Kira spreading destructive information about colleagues. There also seemed to be a division between Kira's 'team of five' and 'the rest'. One example was that even though Angelo held 'all staff' celebrations, Kira would take her team of five off for separate celebrations afterwards. Similarly, whenever Angelo sought feedback on potential changes, Kira's group would all express the same view about what should happen – and it would always benefit Kira.

To change the culture, Angelo approached the problem in a few different ways. Firstly, he decided to set a clear strategy and a new team environment. He brought in an external facilitator for a strategy day to get everyone's input on a new direction for the business and to set new behavior standards for team interactions. The day went well and everyone agreed on the new ways they would operate as one team. Similarly, everyone left the day enthusiastic about the new direction and possibilities for revitalizing the business.

To prepare for this change, Angelo had been meeting weekly with his management team and regularly with all those who reported to him. He had established a good working relationship with Kira, asking her about areas that she was an expert in and making himself vulnerable by admitting that he knew little about some of them. However, he didn't feel that she completely trusted him yet. Once the strategy day was over Angelo made time to speak one to one to Kira and the others to ensure that they understood the importance of cooperation and trust for the success of the team and the new direction. His first challenge came in the next management team meeting. Everyone seemed to default back to the 'what's in it for me' approach. Angelo took the time to explain how strong trust and cross team cooperation had helped his last business unit to outperform all the others.

The next challenge came straight after the next staff celebration, when Kira again took her team off for a private one. Angelo called Kira in and explained that her actions were undermining the agreed team behaviors and the 'all together' environment he was trying to create. By this time Kira trusted Angelo enough to reveal the awful experience she had with Michael. Angelo said that he understood and committed to support Kira in changing her approach. He agreed to always raising his concerns with her one-on-one and not using this issue to undermine her with others. He pointed out that this was one of the agreed team behaviors. In making this undertaking Angelo could also let Kira know that spreading destructive information about colleagues was unacceptable – without having to accuse Kira of doing it.

Angelo then got agreement from the management team to make some structural changes which would mix up the old teams. He continued to raise issues directly with the people concerned, and held them accountable to the agreed standards. The new direction for the business really began to produce results, allowing Angelo to reward the team with public recognition and some with pay rises. In hindsight, Kira could see that Michael and his approach had been the problem which had caused a toxic workplace culture, and Angelo had shown her a much better way to 'win'.

There are several elements in this example that combine to help generate trust in a team through good communication. We now want to look at these five in a bit more detail:

1. understanding people through listening
2. developing people through mentoring
3. developing people through feedback (including negative/constructive feedback)
4. focusing on the bigger picture
5. providing clarity

1. Genuine Listening

Can there be trust where there is no genuine communication? There is no genuine communication without openness to what the other person is saying. This is often neglected in the workplace. It's not just about what we say, it's just as important to understand and engage with the responses. This point is made very well in Stephen Covey's famous statement: "Most people do not listen with the intent to understand; they listen with the intent to reply."[30]

Good communication requires being genuinely interested in people, being empathetic, open and engaged. You need to focus on each person you are listening to, so when they speak you really hear them as a person, not just the words they say. Good communication involves placing yourself at the service of your team and asking what they need to know and feel. Angelo was able to connect well with Kira by having the good of the overall organization at heart, and by really listening to Kira, to address her concerns. You can send signals that you really want to understand by doing things like repeating back. For example: "just to see if I have understood correctly, what you're saying is…" You can also avoid being defensive when someone critiques your ideas, remaining open and discussing how it could be improved. This vulnerability (being prepared to learn from your mistakes) was discussed in chapter two, but it is also an important basis for good communication – particularly when you need to point out mistakes to your team. For your people to be open to the feedback, you need to communicate well and constructively, and your listeners must feel supported, including what is often referred to as psychological safety[31]: *a shared belief that the team is safe for interpersonal risk taking.[32]* This requires you to have a good level of empathy, a sensitivity to body language, and a willingness to be vulnerable in front of others.

2. Developing People Through Mentoring

The idea of a manager as a mentor (or a coach) is very popular.[33] One reason for this popularity is that many people enjoy their work more if they have opportunities to learn. As their manager, you have the opportunity to develop your people and provide them with opportunities to grow. Another reason is the amount of time that people spend working. It is important to most people that they can talk about what is happening in their lives with those who share a large part of their week with them. Not to do so puts people under stress – and it is not until recently that we have become more familiar with the harmful effects of stress and mental illness in the workplace. Having someone to talk to about problems, challenges and uncertainties can be very helpful to someone who is struggling in some way. This leads us to consider how we can develop people through providing feedback.

3. Developing People Through Feedback

Any well-ordered system has a developed structure of positive and negative feedback. To maintain an equilibrium, there is action and reaction to the factors governing performance – things have to be tweaked. The role of a manager is to do this by providing this feedback. Positive and negative feedback are needed to ensure that there is continuous improvement and clarity of both the goals you are looking to achieve and the acceptable means of achieving those goals. Although it is called negative feedback here, it is often referred to as constructive feedback, because it is pointing out an area that needs improvement. Negative feedback should not be delivered in a negative way (tone, body language etc.), but as an opportunity to improve. By providing frequent, specific, low-stakes feedback one-on-one, you will help to keep people motivated and growing. Angelo ensured regular communication with Kira, asking her opinion about areas that Kira was an expert in, thereby building a relationship of open feedback between them.

When considering feedback, all of your casual interactions and getting to know people pay their dividends. Would the person you need to provide feedback to prefer it to be public or private? Would they prefer it to be in front of the team or one-on-one? Most people would prefer negative feedback in private – but what about positive feedback? Surprisingly, not everyone enjoys being praised in public, and this is something you will only find out by getting to know them. Another important consideration is the ratio of feedback you are providing. When you have to provide negative feedback to someone, it can be better received when you have been regularly providing positive feedback as well. Ironically, negative feedback seems to be provided most often, even though it is considered the most difficult to give. It's useful to remind yourself to give positive feedback – through a note to yourself to catch people doing a good job, or by putting an item to celebrate at the top of every agenda (mentally, if not in writing). Some managers have a goal of providing five minutes of informal feedback to every team member every week. This can be a very useful practice for making small suggestions that motivate (positive) or prevent issues escalating (negative). It also makes feedback less 'high risk' because people are used to it.

How you receive feedback yourself sets an example for your team. Do you invite your team to provide you with feedback? If so, how do you react when it is negative? Hopefully not like the manager in the following example!

Example – A Bad Reaction

Rod was the CEO and was asking his direct reports why profit was down. Peter gave the real answer – because last year Rod had decided to lower the price on a large 4-year contract in order to get the sale (and increase his sales bonus). Although Peter put it diplomatically, and didn't refer to the sales bonus, Rod went ballistic. A full 10 minutes of verbal abuse was hurled at Peter, accusing his team of slackness, inefficiency and incompetence.

That was the last time Rod received any genuine feedback. In addition, any feedback Rod gave was seen as unjust criticism. As well as losing money that year, Rod lost all of his senior managers to other organizations and gained the reputation in the industry as a bully.

The alternative to this approach is to seek to understand the feedback that is provided to you. By using feedback, you can learn a great deal more about yourself, identifying issues and increasing your self-awareness and effectiveness. In team meetings you can ask what people think of a suggested way forward and then really listen to the response – the words, the tone and the body language. Similarly, be mindful of your own body language when listening. It is all too easy to send a signal of shutting down, of being too busy or distracted. Maintaining eye contact, siting forward when people speak conveys interest and openness. Having your mobile phone and laptop turned off (or left outside) can show that your full attention is devoted to the people in the room.

Giving Negative Feedback

When you must provide negative feedback, how will you give it and what do you want to achieve? Are you correcting a lack of skill or a poor attitude? The difference is crucial. In the example of Kira and Angelo, Kira had the skill, but it was the attitude that Angelo wanted to change. In your own conversations, using open questions at the outset can ensure that you have all the information you need, and can confirm the version of events that you have received. You can take some time to consider how much the person has been progressing, as well as how far they still have to go. You can think about whether there have been any external pressures on the person and if that is an appropriate question to ask in these circumstances. It can also be useful to keep in mind that even if someone has a 'difficult personality', it is possible to change this. A 2022 study found that people who actively work to change their personality are largely successful, and that most people don't want to see themselves as 'bad'.[34]

Once you are clear on what you would like to say, you can consider how the person is likely to react, how they will receive the message. As a result of your feedback, you will often want action to be taken. You can think about what that action should be, and how you will monitor progress. In Angelo's case, he wanted 'Kira's team' to become part of 'our team'. Angelo had to be clear about the messages that Kira was sending and how they impacted on the goal of having the whole organization working together. Angelo had to consider how best to get Kira engaged in the solution and also to minimize any fear of failure Kira may have had.

What are some specific ways to give negative feedback? Generally, negative feedback conversations work better when you have a plan. Take time to establish the facts so that you know as much as possible about the circumstances. Try to have concrete examples where possible. This will allow you to go into the conversation with a short list of things that you know and things that need clarification. Have things clear in your own mind before trying to explain it to someone else. Information alone doesn't always lead to action – you need to consider the emotions involved. You can think about what you will do if the conversation goes smoothly, and if it goes badly. You can then take some time to consider whether the conversation is going to be constructive and deliver the outcome you need. Finally, after going through this process, remind yourself that you need to have an open mind. You have established what has gone on, and what needs to change to the best of your ability with the information available. However, in that meeting, you may still receive a new piece of information that puts everything into a different perspective. That's fine – you can change the plan, or you can even say that because of the new information you would like to take some time to consider the best way forward and suggest meeting again in the next day or so.

4. Focusing on the Big Picture

Angelo was able to refocus the attention of everyone on the larger context. If the business as a whole has a good plan and an agreed set of values, it helps to remind everyone that their success is part of a larger picture. It is common in organizations to have people focusing on their own success. In the long term however, success is only sustainable if the organization succeeds. By drawing Kira's attention back to this wider goal, Angelo could get everyone striving for the same overall goal. You can do the same thing with your team. Have an overall team goal. Explain what success will mean for everybody involved. You can even spend time with your team developing a set of behavior standards that reflect the culture that your team want to have.

Another role of the context in your discussions with your people is to include what their work means to the larger organization. It is very helpful for people to realize that they are part of achieving the goals of the organization. It can also be useful to explain your own situation. Don't be afraid to show some vulnerability[35] by acknowledging when someone in your team is the expert in a particular area. Another aspect of vulnerability is to explain that some things are outside of your control, and therefore what limitations are placed on you. As a manager in an organization, you do not have unlimited capacity to change the way things are. To balance this, you can also relay problems identified by your team to more senior management. You can seek to have things changed, and you can keep your team up to date on the progress of your efforts. This shows your team that you are prepared to put yourself on the line to help improve things for your team.

It is also helpful to update your team on other things that are happening in the wider organization. You will probably have to attend regular meetings with your own manager. Reporting back on what is happening helps your team to feel connected and informed. However, be sure not to share any information that you have been asked to keep confidential. A lack of communication can lead to demotivation. If people feel that they are not getting the information that they need, they will turn to other sources. Those sources are usually not as accurate and you can end up with rumors affecting people negatively. Rumors are best countered by giving people accurate information in a timely way.

Example: The Rumor Mill

Jacquie worked in a large IT company with many different service contracts for large organizations and government departments. She had come from a competing company and it surprised her to find everyone in the team she managed getting really anxious and distracted in December. Being new she asked one of her team members who knew her from the previous company. He said, "Yeah, I was surprised too, but they restructure some part of the company every six months, but December is the big one." Jacquie decided to raise the issue at her next team meeting and was disturbed at the negative sentiment and concern for their jobs that her team expressed. She went to her manager to get some advice about how to handle the loss of productivity that was apparent. Alan's advice was: "Because people are concerned and unclear about whether our business unit will be affected, they all pass on any scrap of information to each other. I would suggest that you say at your next team meeting that you have spoken to me, and our business unit is trading well. We are not expecting to make any major changes this year." Jacquie felt an almost physical sense of relief in the room when she passed on the message. From then on, she would keep an eye out for the concerned whisperings and indirect questions about the future, so that she could set the record straight and avoid all that lost energy and motivation.

She told me that what really impressed her staff was that one year her business unit was going to be affected. By that time, she had developed a strong relationship with her team and had spoken to all of them about their career aspirations. She called a meeting and told everyone that there were going to be changes, but that she thought the changes could be managed so that no one would lose their job. She finished by saying that she would make a time to speak to people one-on-one to identify any cost savings, and finished by saying "If anything changes, I will let you know." Because Jacquie had been mentoring some of her team, when the changes came through one person was promoted to another department and no one lost their job. She gained a lot of respect and from that point on, people would come and ask her if they heard any rumors, and productivity did not take a dip every six months!

5. Providing Clarity

As you can see in the example of Jacquie, one of your key roles as a manager is to think systematically, which facilitates clarity, allowing you to see the consequences of various options – both in terms of resources and outcomes but more importantly, in terms of the people in your team. Considering people's strengths means that you actually have to know them. So walking the line of being personal and approachable and at the same time avoiding being overly familiar is an important consideration. When this line is clear, communications are clear, expectations are clear and goals are clear. When people understand the thought processes behind the goals, they tend to own those processes – they have 'buy in' and ownership of the outcomes.

Example: The Puppeteer

Luke was working in a government department. His manager, Kevin, believed that 'knowledge is power' and shared as little information as he could. Kevin's team were working on a proposal that could significantly change how healthcare was delivered. However, because Kevin wanted to be the only one who understood how each part fitted together, each team member was working in isolation. They were not supposed to share their work with their colleagues because Kevin was the proposal 'owner'. They would each write their section of the proposal and submit it to Kevin for approval. The corrections that were returned to them seemed disconnected from what they had been asked to do. The repeated, seemingly pedantic corrections left the team feeling disempowered and frustrated. Luke started applying for transfers and had left by the time Kevin finally submitted 'his' proposal. It did not surprise Luke that the proposal was strongly criticized for being too disjointed. Some parts emphasized the monetary savings and others emphasized patient outcomes, but no section considered both.

This example illustrates the dangers of team members not knowing the ultimate goal of the work they do. You as a manager can decide how much to share, depending on the specific project and the number of moving parts. But at least all members of the team should know where their work, and even their personal goals, fit in with and contribute to the overarching goal. You can consider whether the information is better delivered individually or to the team together.

https://dominicmcloughlin.com/

Having considered these five important elements of communication, we now want to move onto consider the 'how'. What is the best way to communicate? What about the move to virtual teams or hybrid teams? Let's have a look at these two questions now.

Spontaneous or Deliberate?

A common recommendation for communicating with your team is to be spontaneous. However, another is that you need to be deliberate or purposeful in your interactions. This can cause confusion, because they seem to be at opposite ends of the communication spectrum. So how can you do both? The solution to this conundrum is not to ask 'which one should I do?', but rather 'when and where'? Different times and circumstances call for different responses. You can also be deliberate about what you want to do, but spontaneous about when and how. For example, if there was some news about a new client, you can decide how to tell your team. You could call everyone together first thing in the morning and announce it, or you can tell people as you naturally encounter them throughout the day. Similarly, there can be a big difference in the message you convey when you ask people to catch up over a coffee in a meeting room, versus asking them to come into your office. Taking a moment to consider these factors can help you be more intentional, and more reflective, about your communication.

It is also a good habit to develop a general friendliness towards the people that you meet. Even just smiling and saying hello to those you encounter is surprisingly powerful for facilitating communication. We are always measuring faces by their 'responsiveness' – which essentially means openness – even without thinking. Empathy is a prerequisite for effective communication – and this means knowing how to really listen – to what people say, and what they don't say. Listening to someone telling you about their weekend may seem like wasted time, but in reality, it is building an important relationship which facilitates good communication. Don't forget that you will want people to listen to you!

Communicating Virtually

Although the pandemic has made remote working more common, it has also highlighted some of the difficulties of maintaining a cohesive team when the team never gather together in the same place. All of the things covered so far in this chapter are more difficult when a person works remotely, but they are still vital.[36]

The first thing to consider when managing remote workers is how you will measure performance. When managing most people, it is better to look at the outcomes, rather than to try and micromanage every element of the process. With advances in information technology, there is often the capacity for managers to measure things like time spent 'online', but you have to ask yourself what you are trying to achieve. As long as you are getting the things you need, on time and of a good quality, do you need to be concerned about the time spent online? Many of us spend time thinking about a problem while walking or driving, so being 'online' is not a great measure of the work that was done. Generally speaking, it is better to trust that the person is doing the work, if the outcomes are satisfactory. The alternative is you spending a lot of time trying to use digital surveillance and 'measures' to catch someone out.

Speaking of technology, it is worth taking some time to consider the tools provided to your remote team members. Do they have the right equipment and sufficient training in the tools you use? Similarly, consider how you can use things like video and phone conferencing to ensure that offsite team members are able to participate as much as possible with the other team members. Regular check-ins, team meetings and work in progress discussions can really help a virtual workforce to feel a part of the organization. Likewise, taking the time to share good news, and your appreciation for the efforts of remote team members really helps the team culture you are trying to generate.

Although communication might need some more thought and planning, it is important to ensure that you are attuned to the remote team member. Do they prefer phone or video? Is an email better for some things? How would you prefer that they communicate with you? You also need to have times that you are available for the remote team member. Remember, too that you lead by example, not emailing or calling outside of normal working hours. You don't want to pressure a remote worker to be 'always available'.

Some managers use an email designation in the subject line to help with virtual communication – examples are 'for consultation', 'for action', 'social news'. During the pandemic, many workplaces started having a virtual Friday afternoon social gathering where no discussion of work was allowed. Other social ideas included the game Pictionary, but using a shared screen to paint (called Paintionary). Some people went for a walk in their own local area while chatting to colleagues walking in their area.

Others had a 'virtual workspace' where people could work quietly together for an hour or two. This had the advantage of working alongside colleagues, and being able to ask questions as they arose of others who were in the virtual room. Another idea is assigning an in office 'buddy' to a remote worker. The person in the office undertakes to keep the remote worker up to date with anything happening and is available to answer any questions the buddy may have. There are a lot of different ways to build a strong team that includes remote team members. It is about remembering that this will require a bit more planning on your part.

Two lessons from virtual meetings are related to the material covered in this chapter already. First, choose the relevant people to invite. It is tempting to invite more people to online meetings, but this can be counter-productive. A smaller group of people who are genuinely interested seems to provide better results. Second, establish the rules for your online team meetings. To maximize engagement it seems that 'video on' and 'no multitasking' are minimum requirements for your team rules. So it might take a bit more effort to achieve meaningful virtual communication, but the principles discussed in this chapter are still very relevant.

As we saw in chapter three, taking a genuine interest in your people is essential to building trust and outstanding performance. The interactions with your team are important to assist you and your team in working together. These interactions also assist in deciding how to delegate. Delegation is something of an art form because you challenge people, to increase their capability, but you don't want to overwhelm them. Delegation also builds trust, but this time it requires a level of trust from you. After all, trust is a two-way street. If we want people to trust us, we also have to show that we trust them. Before moving onto that chapter, consider how you can improve your communication through the exercise below.

Start your journey with just 5 minutes a day

Day 1: Reflect on your strengths and weaknesses in communicating one-on-one with your team members.

Day 2: Choose one thing from this chapter to try today that would improve on one thing from your Day 1 reflection.

Day 3: Reflect on your strengths and weaknesses in communicating your team as a group.

Day 4: Choose one thing from this chapter to try today that would improve on one thing from your Day 3 reflection.

Day 5: Reflect on the ratio of positive to negative/constructive feedback you give. What can you do next week to improve this?

Chapter 7:

Application – Delegation

©dominicmcloughlin.com

<u>In this Chapter:</u>

- Why Delegate?
- Assessing the Task
- Supporting
- Setting Realistic Expectations
- Example of How Not to Delegate

In the next two chapters, we apply all the principles contained in the previous chapters to delegation and decision making. Delegation is needed because your role is facilitating the work of the team. You don't have enough time to do everything yourself! Second, as we saw in the previous chapter, part of developing your people is helping them to grow in knowledge and experience. Giving a team member responsibility for a project (or part of a project) is a great way of doing this. However, it is very important to ensure that your people succeed in these projects, so we spend the rest of the chapter considering how to delegate while also supporting them.

Why Delegate?

Being a manager rarely has an obvious short-term payoff. Deadlines, obstacles and crises seem to alternate in an endless cycle, creating one of the major difficulties for any manager – the sense of not having enough time. Many organizations will be focused on your ability to bring in (or keep) clients, to be profitable, to deliver the goods (or services). The key measures through which you are assessed rarely include your interactions with your team. These are all factors which make it easy to focus on the latest crisis or decision. Retreating from the team can seem necessary to get things done.

However, good managers are in reality good delegators. Good managers engage with their team to deliberately develop their skills. This allows your team to handle more tasks and make more decisions. This then frees you up for your actual role.

The role of a manager is facilitating the work of those who are doing the tasks – not doing the tasks yourself.

It is very easy to fall back into doing the tasks yourself, because the tasks are familiar, clear and time pressured, but this is a mistake. The survey showed that the best managers were good at delegating. They delegated both authority and responsibility appropriately, taking into consideration the distinct personalities, backgrounds and motivations of team members.

An Example of Not Delegating

Keith was a bit of a perfectionist. No-one in his team could do things as well as he could. He was proud of his reputation with clients for his top-class social media and website management. He had trouble believing that any of his team of 10 could do the work as well as he could. He had given Aimee a report to do around six months before, and it didn't go well. Keith thought Aimee had been around long enough to know how he worked, so he gave her the task and said "It's a straightforward report – just do it the way I normally do." Keith gave her plenty of space to get on with it, but she didn't seem to know what he wanted. Eventually he realized he would have to check on her every day, which meant that he spent so much time checking her work, he may as well have done it himself. As for the rest of the team, he really questioned their motivation. They always seemed to be joking around on the odd occasions that he left his office.

The amount of digital work exploded when the lockdowns started and, although he got on well with his regular clients, there were now many clients that he had never met in person. Keith was complaining about some of the new clients while grabbing a quick coffee with his team – these new clients seemed quite unreasonable in their demands for their work to be delivered, but they wouldn't acknowledge the pressure everyone was under. A couple of the team members in the break room offered to take the more obnoxious clients for him, but Keith resisted. He didn't think they were as committed to the quality of the work as he was.

One month later, it all became too much for Keith. After working all weekend, he came in early on Monday, only to find another stack of abusive emails from the troublesome clients. His team was astonished to find him sobbing at his desk. Everyone was very concerned for him and suggested he take some time off. Keith's manager was notified. Keith eventually recovered, but it took a couple of months, and in the meantime, no one really knew how to fill in for him, which caused several clients to take their business elsewhere.

Keith made a few classic errors in this example. He assumed Aimee would know what he wanted. He didn't offer assistance, but left her to work it out. Then, when she could not duplicate his preferred method, he changed to micromanagement – checking on every aspect of the work she was doing. Keith also spent too much time in his office, not getting to know his team and seeing what they were interested in working on. In assuming no-one could do the work as well as he could, Keith didn't provide professional development, and he also stopped the business from having anyone to fill in for him. Finally, this example also illustrates the long-term risks to your wellbeing of trying to do everything yourself, so let's have a look at delegating appropriately.

Balancing Workloads

You are responsible for ensuring that everything that needs to be done is done. At the same time, you want to try to share out the tasks in a way that is fair. You don't want some of your people to be burned out while others don't have enough to do – both of which most people find demotivating. It is also damaging to trust when work is distributed unfairly. Delegating tasks to team members also frees up your time to focus on more strategic questions, which is itself very valuable.[37] Finally, delegating allows your people to develop in their own careers through the valuable learning and growth opportunities that greater responsibility brings.

Assessing the Task or Project

Firstly, you need to assess whether a task or project can be delegated, taking into consideration the various team members and their suitability. (We use 'task' from here on for ease of reading).

DON'T:

– Delegate the recruitment of people
– Delegate the management of poor performance

Because these two areas are key to your team's success, and because they require a knowledge of how the entire team works, they should be done by the manager.

<u>DO build trust through:</u>

a. Knowing the strengths and weaknesses of your people and delegating things that fit with their strengths

Wanting the best for your people also means that you want them to succeed. Ensure that you are delegating something that will stretch the person, but not break them.

b. Considering the career aspirations of the person you are thinking of delegating to

Assigning a project to someone who would like to become a manager one day is an excellent learning opportunity for them. However, that is not everyone's aspiration.

c. Acknowledging when a team member has more expertise than you in a particular area

Some of your team may be more expert in an area than you. This is a great opportunity to be humble enough to acknowledge that expertise by asking them to undertake a task in that area. This approach is likely to produce a better outcome and to help build trust. Your conversations and efforts to get to know your team (covered in the earlier chapters) will help you to know what people are looking to do.

Supporting

You have the opportunity to demonstrate your trust in the person you are delegating to.

DON'T

– delegate a task and just 'leave them to it'

This is not effective delegation and often results in disappointing outcomes for all concerned.

– micromanage[38]

The best focus is the end goal – that is what is important. They should be free to experiment in how they would like to get to that goal, rather than just do it the way that you would do it. You want to demonstrate your trust in the person.

DO build trust through:

d.   Providing a good background and summary of the context

Understanding the various stakeholders and how the problem came about is useful for avoiding misunderstandings. It also ensures that relevant parties will be consulted on any proposed solutions.

e.   Explaining what has to be achieved (goal/outcome)

Being clear about the goal helps to ensure that the task or project meets your objective. Explain what you would see as a success. If it doesn't meet the need that you have, then the delegation doesn't help you or the team.

f.   Outlining the resources available

You are also responsible for ensuring that the person has the appropriate resources to complete the task – time, money or people.

Include the fact that you are prepared to help with advice and your time. You should also offer any additional training needed to address a skill or knowledge gap.

g.   Stipulating the authority being given

This may be authority to manage someone else assigned to the task or to spend a certain amount of money to time, or to forego some of the other work that they normally do. It is important to consider this in advance and then to discuss it with the person prior to beginning the project, so that you are both clear on what is expected.

h.   Scheduling progress reports

Regular opportunities to discuss how the task is going are essential for both of you. You will need to be clear about how often you will meet up to check on progress and provide mentoring or advice.

Setting Realistic Expectations

Clear communication about your expectations is vital. You don't want to micromanage, but you want to be available when needed. In larger organizations, a person may be part of your team but also be involved in other project groups. How much time a person has to dedicate to various tasks and projects is an important factor for consideration. Where there is a lack of clarity around these areas, conflicts and misunderstandings can easily arise. The section on clarity of communication in the previous chapter is very relevant here.

DON'T

—   Assume the person knows what you expect

Providing clear guidelines about the standard of the work to be delivered can be helpful. Thinking about the amount of progress you would expect to see for each progress report can help ensure expectations are clear. Regular opportunities to discuss how the task is going are essential for both of you.

—   Assume that there will not be any obstacles

Discussing in advance any obstacles that you envisage can help give some guidance about how problems should be dealt with.

DO build trust through:

i.   Providing guidelines about when you should be brought in.

Some things to consider are: a stakeholder is being obstructive, a problem is likely to delay the project by x amount of time, or cost x amount of money.

j.   Allowing for the fact that this person is learning

As discussed in chapter three, this is where your patience and tolerance for mistakes is needed. Trying different ways of doing things (being innovative) can lead to excellent results, but it can also have problems along the way. Seeing delegation as part of developing your people gives you the opportunity to patiently provide feedback and mentoring.

k.   Providing positive feedback

Show your appreciation when something is done well. Even if a task isn't being completed as quickly as you would have liked, you can still offer encouragement and constructive criticism. Your feedback will help to improve the person's capacity to undertake a similar task next time.

l.   Giving credit

Be sure to give credit to the person who has undertaken the task. Others in the organization will hear about the great work that they have done and it will help build the person's confidence. It also builds their trust in you, and of course, loyalty.

m. Conducting a post-mortem

Reflecting on what went well and what needed improvement is a good way for a person to consolidate the lessons from this experience. Discussing it also allows you to give your perspective on how things went – outlining a 'management perspective' which is also a learning opportunity for the person to whom you delegated the task. You can also get feedback on how well your delegation worked from the team member's perspective.

In Summary

At the end of this process, what have you gained? You will have had someone else complete something that you would otherwise have had to do. More importantly, a member of your team has grown in their own capacity to manage tasks and projects. You have demonstrated your trust in your people while providing a genuine development opportunity. Your team will see that you are genuinely helping them to develop as people and in their careers. As well as developing a team that you can rely on to get things done, you will also see that delegation can generate new ideas for the way things are done. Over time, the increased innovation, capacity, and trust will deliver outstanding performance for your team.

Example: How Not to Delegate

Jessica was happy co-ordinating the delivery of some health services for a local region and she was widely acknowledged as doing an excellent job. Her manager moved to another city, leaving the website administration role vacant. The local management team asked Jess if she would be happy to take on the website administration role while they recruited a new manager, and Jess agreed. Interviews were conducted, but three months passed and nothing happened. Jessica approached the management team to ask what was happening, as she was doing two jobs and wanted a resolution. The response she received was: "Oh – we thought you would keep doing it." Jess pointed out that she had agreed to do it for a short time temporarily and asked about the interview candidates. This resulted in someone finally being appointed to fill the role, but within weeks, that replacement was seconded to another area. Finally, after 12 months of having too much to do, Jess was burned out and approached the management team again. Amazingly the response was the same as before: "We thought you could keep doing it." Jessica resigned from the web administration role, effective immediately.

What went wrong here, in terms of what we've been discussing? There are a number of the DO's that were absent. No one in the management team discussed Jess' career aspirations. They could have found out early on that she had no wish to be promoted permanently. There was no attempt to explain what the outcome was. If the goal had been a handover in 3 months' time, Jess would have known what to expect, and the recruitment would have been taken much more seriously. Regular progress reports would have shown that Jess was feeling overwhelmed, enabling additional support to be provided. Similarly, if someone had been allocated to support Jessica, they would have realized how much work was really involved and enabled the management team to understand that she would not continue doing two roles indefinitely. Some positive feedback on what a great job Jess was doing, along with appointing someone to assist her, could have encouraged her to decide to take the promotion. Part of the problem was that the 'management team' all thought that someone else was looking after it. In reality, no one was. They could have designated one person as her manager which would have meant that they took the responsibility for Jess seriously and enabled clearer communication.

There were also some DO NOT's that should have been avoided. The task was delegated and Jess was just left to it. The management team assumed Jess knew what they were thinking and expecting. The management team did not check if there were any obstacles to Jess doing the work, or their plan for her to continue in the role. All of these could have been avoided.

In our survey,[39] the best managers delegated authority and responsibility appropriately, however, the worst managers were described as being very 'hands off'. They delegated all the work and did not dedicate any of their time to help manage the workload (similar to the example of Jessica above). Some of the worst managers relied on control and surveillance, rather than trusting their people. They took an approach of 'looking over shoulders' and micromanaging, demanding that they be the ones to approve every decision. The survey participants stated that this created a harsh work environment that led to resentment and low morale.

Micromanagement, control, and surveillance undermine trust. As we have seen, high levels of trust are built in a professional relationship where both parties trust each other. The best managers trusted their team members to work autonomously to deliver the work without micromanaging. Instead, they set the expectations, provided the necessary resources, and then allowed team members to decide on their own work processes. A clear outline of what is to be done and by when allows you to trust your team to get the task or project completed in whatever way suits them, but also holds people accountable for completing the work. This form of delegation, with support and progress reports, allows for important innovations to appear. At the same time, it allows people to make, and learn from, mistakes giving the freedom to grow and improving the performance of individuals and your whole team.

What you decide to delegate, and to whom you delegate, are examples of decisions that are appropriate for you to make. However, research shows that participation by your team members in decisions that affect them leads to greater job satisfaction and feeling trusted.[40] In the next chapter we apply the principles, from the earlier chapters, to an example of decision making in a team meeting. Before moving to that chapter, consider how you can improve your delegation through the exercise below.

Start your journey with just 5 minutes a day

Day 1: Reflect on how much you delegate. Is there more that you could be giving to your team members?

Day 2: Choose one thing from this chapter to try today that would improve on one thing from your Day 1 reflection.

Day 3: Reflect on the support you provide those you have delegated work to.

Day 4: Choose one thing from this chapter to try today that would improve on one thing from your Day 3 reflection.

Day 5: Reflect on what you have learned from trying these things. Are there any lessons to learn? What can you do next week?

Chapter 8:

Application – Decision Making

©dominicmcloughlin.com

<u>In this Chapter:</u>

- Poor Decision Making
- How Not to Decide
- What the Best Managers Do
- Five Stages of Good Decision Making
- Practical Application – Using the Five Stages

We saw in the previous chapter that it is challenging to balance the competing demands on you. Decision making is another complex area which requires careful balancing. Some of the tensions most managers grapple with are:

- feeling short of time, but knowing that consultation with the team improves decision making;
- carrying the responsibility for a decision, but wanting to give the team a say;
- wanting the best solutions, yet dreading the conflict about what the best solution is.

There is no shortage of advice, in fact there are more books on decision making than could be read in a lifetime.[41] In this chapter we want to focus on keeping it simple. by considering the main stages of a meeting, and then using a real-life example to illustrate the approach of the best managers. As we go through this chapter, we will highlight some of the connections to the earlier chapters in this book.

Let's begin with an example of poor decision making and then consider what went wrong.

Example – Poor Decision Making

When Simon's fantastic principal retired, he immediately noticed the difference. This principal was known for his ability to pull the staff together – he was a living testament to good management. In the changes that followed, Bruce, the sports teacher, was promoted to deputy principal. Instead of wearing the hallmark shorts and team polo shirt, Bruce immediately started wearing a shirt and tie. Within weeks, a new policy was issued for comment, requiring all teachers to wear a shirt and tie. Sport teachers were exempt. Simon and the other woodwork teachers suggested that some other subjects should also be exempt, due to the nature of the teaching environment. In his case, a hot workshop with a lot of sawdust, etc. No discussion or meeting took place, the policy was finalized and released with no changes, none of the comments were addressed.

At the end of the first week of the new policy being in effect, Simon was told that he would have a disciplinary meeting on Monday to discuss his lack of compliance with the new policy. Bruce was shocked to find that Simon brought along a legal representative who insisted that the new policy was unreasonable. After much discussion, Bruce was forced to agree to additional exemptions for some teachers and felt that he had been publicly embarrassed. Simon resigned soon after.

How Not to Decide

So, what went wrong? There were a number of missteps that are very common when moving from managing a team you know well, to a team that does not know you.

Bruce showed in his change of 'uniform' that he had changed his role and his outlook on how he should represent himself. However, he didn't stop to think that others may not have made the same adjustment, or that they may need time to do so. All of the staff at the school were now part of Bruce's team, but he proposed a policy change as if he was still in charge of physical education – he gave his former team an exemption, but did not extend that exemption to others who had previously had it. In fact, he divided his new team, by referencing his old team.

Bruce also made his decision without consultating those who were affected. He issued a new policy and asked for comments on it, rather than seeking the team's ideas about how professionalism could be improved and then issuing a policy based on the discussions. He also ignored the genuine issues that were raised about the new policy and pushed ahead with his preferred solution. He also failed to check on the legal requirements before pushing ahead with his idea.

Having failed to properly consult the people affected by his decision, Bruce was surprised by the level of resistance and resentment that he encountered. Because he underestimated the legitimacy of the complaints and the amount of opposition, he was forced to back down and reverse his first major decision.

Some of these mistakes are highlighted in the survey findings too. Some of the worst managers made poor decisions because of inexperience. Many of the worst managers barely involved their people in deciding, and some of those decisions had very detrimental effects on the team. Others knew that the idea had been unsuccessful before, but the manager didn't because they didn't ask anyone. Finally, the worst managers often made poor decisions by allowing undue emotion to interfere with the process.

What do the best managers do?

By contrast, the best managers avoided these traps by listening to various perspectives, being genuinely open to suggestions, and planning for things to go wrong. The best managers avoided becoming attached to a particular solution, allowing them to make more informed decisions. They also carefully considered the impact on the people involved, as well as the business.

Good Decision Making

In order to apply the practices of the best managers, we now go through the various stages of a decision-making process. Although this is only one approach, it has been shown to be effective. After going through the stages, we will then apply these same stages to a real-life decision, so that you can see how it works in practice.

Stage One: Initial Planning

This first stage is often overlooked, but is very beneficial. It involves consideration of the nature of the problem and whether there are benefits to involving your team in generating possible solutions.

    a.   Identify the problem

Some problems can be solved once, and that solution can then be reused. Other problems, however, have to be managed by being revisited as they constantly develop. In our environment of increased change and uncertainty these dynamic problems are becoming much more common. Managers are having to face more dynamic decision-making processes than before. It can be frustrating for all concerned when a 'once and for all' solution, applied in a one-off situation, is implemented for a developing issue, because it will just resurface.

Similarly, the nature of the problem may influence which model or system of problem solving might be most appropriate. Taking the time in your initial planning to consider how you will work through the problem can help you use the time for the meeting itself much more effectively.

Finally, the nature of the problem can influence whether you should consult your entire team. That may not always be the case. Your understanding of your team members, the sort of decision being made and the potential impact on your team are all useful criteria for considering the positives and negatives of team participation in a decision. Sometimes you may select participants based on the expertise required or on the availability of team members.

b.   Set a procedure for the meeting

Once you have decided that you need to have team members present to help solve a problem, most meetings are assisted by setting an agenda. Depending on the decision, some discussions will need the visionary style – the big picture people, those more concerned about the effect on staff, those more interested in the details and those who are more interested in the action items.[42] These are all needed, but they are not all needed for every decision, or at every stage of a discussion. Explaining that the process will ensure that everyone gets to contribute in line with their strengths can avoid frustration

c. Arrange the meeting

The final stage of your initial planning is to consider where and when you will hold the meeting to discuss the issue. Some decisions can be included in a regular team meeting, whereas others will require dedicated time to reach a conclusion.

There is also the question of whether a dedicated meeting should be in person or virtual. There are advantages to having everyone there in person, as it is easier to read body language and have side conversations, for example. However, meeting virtually is sometimes quicker to set up and can be very effective. [43]

Stage Two: Brief the Team

From your initial planning, you should have a clear outline to present to the team. This briefing can be sent out with the invitation and agenda prior to the meeting, or it can be presented at the start of the meeting itself. The briefing will ideally outline the decision to be made (or the problem to be considered), the end goal, and the timeline for deciding. The end goal is usually something that will benefit the team and/or the organization. Often the goal is related to: making people's jobs easier in the long term (improved efficiency); better communication and coordination (workflow); more sales (profitability); or benefiting a client (better services).

The content of the briefing flows from your initial planning and provides a summary that tries to avoid unnecessary detail on what is already known, but also provides enough information for people to begin thinking about the issue prior to the meeting. For a very complex discussion, some pre-reading may be needed. As mentioned above, you can outline the decision-making process you would like to follow. A common language or a common model can be very helpful for more productive decision making.[44] If you don't have a preferred model (from past meetings or your initial planning) then the 'best model to use' could be the first item on the agenda.

Stage Three: The Meeting

    d.   Allow team discussion, do not lead with your ideas

Once the meeting starts, there are two temptations that all of us suffer from. The first arises from the planning you've done – the temptation to outline the solution that you think would be best. This is usually a bad idea for two main reasons. Firstly, those present at the meeting have not been thinking about the problem for as long, and usually haven't considered all the options that you have. Therefore, the team are not usually committed to what they would see as 'your solution', not 'our solution'. Secondly, because you are the manager, revealing your thoughts first can stifle any discussion of different possibilities. As one experienced manager put it: "I may have identified a 'great' solution, but if my team are only 50% committed to it, I am better off having a 'good' solution with 100% commitment."[45]

The second temptation is to grab at the first solution that is presented. However, the quick, easy and popular answers are often not the best options for the long term. More discussion may well reveal weaknesses in the idea or better alternatives. At the start of the meeting, therefore, it is good to remind people upfront that the discussion is valuable. It is worthwhile asking your team to try to build on the ideas that are suggested, rather than to critique them. It may be useful to ask everyone to suspend judgement in the early phase, while things are being discussed. Ask the team not to shoot down riskier ideas, but rather to ask: "How could this work?"

    e.   Focus discussion on problems and solutions, not participants

Some 'ground rules' may be useful. Statements that help preserve the discussion and avoid conflict between people, but generating robust discussion about ideas. The aim is to maintain a productive tension around solutions, not around the people in the discussion. Emphasizing the importance of openness and collegiality can be helpful. Sometimes, committing to keeping the discussion confidential helps people to feel more able to share their true thoughts.

Most meetings will have some element of conflict, and there is a lot to be gained by constructive conflict around different ideas. However, it needs to remain a conflict of ideas, not degenerate into a conflict between the people proposing the ideas, so be prepared to manage that. Step into a discussion that is getting too heated. Some tactics that can help are: summarizing what each party is saying, noting that both points of view have value, asking if anyone can see a way to incorporate both perspectives.

f.   Ask open questions, maintain energy

One key aspect of your role as a participant in the meeting is to maintain energy. Show that you are confident that a solution will be developed and keep asking open questions. Be curious when some people are under-contributing or over-contributing. At this stage it is all about opening horizons and considering many perspectives. You are not committed to going with any idea, just exploring them thoroughly. You can also observe the dynamics of your team, as well as making progress on an issue. You have an opportunity to leverage the various backgrounds, disciplines, and cultures in your team – generating diversity of thought and more robust decisions. All the while, remembering to practice smiling and thoughtful listening.

Stage Four: Considering Solutions

Once the meeting gets to the point where you have one or two solutions that the team prefers, it is worth mentally 'stepping back' to consider any external factors that may be relevant.

g.   Consider external factors: risks, synergies etc.

Are there any potential synergies with other teams in your organization? Should their input be sought before finally deciding? What about the risks? Identifying the risks allows you to think about how those risks could be managed. This, in turn, allows you to consider the potential downsides of the options.

h.   Identify a small-scale test

For some solutions it is worth considering whether you could try a solution on a small scale first. Maybe with one client, or with one location. This lower risk option may provide an opportunity to see how the solution works in reality and to fine tune the implementation before increasing the scope. Other questions that can help to 'reality check' solutions are: What's the backup plan? What support is needed for the team? What would the impact be further down the line for the team, the organization, or the client? Once all of this has been considered, one option may actually be more attractive than the other.

i.   Make 'who is doing what' clear, including deadlines

As part of discussing solutions, rough out the various tasks that flow from it. Identifying and assigning people who may be best placed to deliver. You want to be sure that the process doesn't finish with everyone thinking that you are going to do everything. This is the likely assumption, unless you clearly communicate what things will be done, by who and by when. It is also an opportunity to reconnect the work of each person to the overall goal that you had at the outset, as it may have gotten lost in the details of the discussion. You also want to avoid the situation where there was discussion and a decision, but nothing happens.

j.   Values check

A last question worth asking is 'should we do this?' Checking against the values of the organization, the team and your own personal code is a great way to ensure that the team sees that you respect these values in reality. In the survey reported in Chapter 2, one of the key points of difference related to this area of values. When thinking of the best manager they had ever had, 75% (881) based their decisions on the 'right thing to do' rather than 'making money'.

Of course, an organization needs to make enough money to continue to operate, to provide jobs to people and goods or services to clients. However, when this becomes the over-riding goal of the business unit or organization, people recognize that the values the organization claims to stand for are not the real priority. When thinking of the worst manager, they had ever had only 11% (129) based their decisions on the 'right thing to do' rather than 'making money'. This difference of 64% between the best and worst managers shows how important living your values, and the values of the organization really is.[46]

Stage Five: Document

The final stage is writing up all of the relevant material and confirming the allocation of people and tasks. Sometimes this happens within the meeting and sometimes afterwards. Whenever it happens, it is important to have a written record of what was decided, who was given a task and when they are required to deliver their work.

Now, we can look at how these stages worked, putting you in the shoes of the manager in this example.

Practical Application – Using the Five Stages

You come away from the meeting with your manager (Ken) and you feel very annoyed. No-one likes it when their boss receives a customer complaint about their team – let alone a whole page of slow response times like the one in your hand. At least Ken had some sympathy: "I know they're difficult to deal with, but we just have to gather our evidence and provide a strong response to this issue." Thankfully you had been prepared with the numbers of calls and escalations that your team has to deal with on a daily basis. Ken has agreed to transfer two additional staff into your team tomorrow to assist.

The whole communication process is problematic, in your opinion. The ultimate customer has a critical rail infrastructure that operates 24 hours a day. But your customer – the consulting company – provides all of the IT services to the rail company. Your organization had been subcontracted to provide many of these services over two years ago: Servers, Networks, Applications and Helpdesk. The only one of these that was within your control was the Networks.

A lot of problems seem to be caused by the unreasonable nature of the contract. Someone had agreed to get the 'duplicate network' online within 10 minutes and big money is at stake any time that doesn't happen. As the network is both old and undergoing an extensive upgrade, the duplicate network is being called upon outside ordinary working hours far too often. In your own team, every time there is a network problem of any description, it is escalated very quickly – in case the duplicate network is needed.

Your inbox is a testament to how ridiculous this has become – over 100 emails a day – copying you in to every network issue 'just in case'.

Tomorrow, when you will be a bit calmer, you will set aside some time early in the morning to consider how to proceed.

Stage One: Initial Planning

Before everyone else comes into work, you start to plan the meeting you need to have.

a.   Identify the problem

The first problem is the list of complaints. You will need to provide an explanation for them to your boss, so that Ken can take them to the client. You find the list of responses your predecessor used when this happened last year.

The bigger problem is that these complaints continue to arise – is there anything that can be done about that? You decide to use a model that your team members are familiar with: First - identify the facts. Second - identify the problems based on those facts. Third – identify possible solutions to those problems.

Finally, you consider who you should consult. The number of incidents and the fact that complaints keep recurring mean that you would like to involve as many of your team members as possible.

b.   Set a procedure for the meeting

You decide to set the agenda as follows:

1. Short-term: addressing the incidents that are part of the complaint: the 'time to resolution' for after-hours calls is too slow
    - Facts, Problems, Solutions
2. Long-term solutions
3. Allocation of Work – Goals, Tasks and Timing

c.   Arrange the meeting

You consider the number of incidents that you need to discuss, and the best way to involve as many of your team as possible. You decide to allocate all of your casual and contract staff to cover for those attending the meeting. Wednesdays seem to be a quieter day than the others, so you set the meeting for Wednesday morning two weeks away. The two additional staff should be up to speed by then, and they can help cover for those attending the meeting. You decide to get everyone to come into the office. You book the large meeting room.

Stage Two: Brief the Team

From your initial planning, you have a clear outline to present to the team. You provide the outline and the agenda to your team via email. Your email concludes with your goals: a long-term reduction in the incidents, better communication with the client, better communication within the team. You send an email to those staff who will be unable to attend, asking them to send any thoughts they have, or to arrange to meet with you, prior to the date of the meeting. In the days between now and the meeting you ensure that you ask each person who cannot attend whether they have any thoughts.

Stage Three: The Meeting

d.   Allow team discussion, do not lead with your ideas

You begin the meeting by outlining the process you want to follow. You state that the issues are complex but solvable. You remind everyone that throughout the meeting you want to maintain a productive discussion. You want to identify the problems and solutions, but there also needs to be agreement on the facts to begin. Although you have some ideas about possible solutions yourself, you ask for the meeting to identify the facts around the first agenda item: the 'time to resolution' for after-hours calls is too slow.

Darren starts and tends to dominate (a point you note, to raise with him later in private). He raises a number of points. He is supported by Adrienne, Pina and Luis who are also very vocal. You note the concerns about:

- long hours of work and the amount of pressure on the team
- the unfairness of the contract

Karen and Tony raise:

- low morale, mostly due to backlog of work and inequitable distribution of workload

You notice that Naimh, Maxine, George haven't said much and you invite their contribution. They raise two further issues:

- no opportunity to be pro-active
- need for improved communication in the change management process

Having allowed everyone to have a chance to vent their frustrations, you ask if it's possible to outline the facts that underpin these issues. You are able to list the following:

-   In the last three months there was an average of 93 logged calls per month for the network support staff, with 12 outside ordinary working hours. Therefore, there is an average of three after-hours callouts every week. Some weeks were busy and others quiet, depending on the amount of work the consulting firm is doing on the Network.
-   Average fix time is two hours per network resolution
-   The consulting firm pays a fixed amount per month for all of the Network Management. After hours support is Included. Profit for the contract is sitting at 11%, already below the 15% company standard
-   The 'change management process' has to have final sign-off before a problem is considered 'resolved'
-   The average time taken from submission to the consultants to sign off by the client is 45 minutes

In the problem stage the following are identified:

-   After hours payment is too low, for the amount of work required. People are reluctant to be on the after-hours roster because of this. Those who are on the roster are becoming burned out. George thinks that the Server team get double.
-   Accessing the secure network with administration privileges requires a complex set of steps, leading to delays.

- The change management process (designed by the consulting firm) is inefficient, having too many people involved in it

You thank everyone for their efforts in identifying the main problems that need to be resolved and suggest a break before reconvening to move onto the solutions stage.

When you all return, you ask if anyone has thought of any factors that have been missed in your first session. Darren starts complaining about the unfairness of the contract again. You point out that you can raise that issue with Ken, but for the moment, the contract cannot be changed.

You remind everyone that you are moving into the solutions phase and ask that everyone suspend judgement while things are being discussed: "Rather than see the problems in a suggestion, let's begin by asking 'how could this work?'"

e.   Focus discussion on problems and solutions, not participants

Karen raises the suggestion of putting dedicated staff on the documentation backlog. Darren says "Who's going to do that – it's too big and too boring – we don't have time anyway." Karen responds – well what's your great idea then? It's obvious says Darren – we just have to get more money for the after-hours work. You decide to step into the discussion that is getting too personal. You remind everyone of the importance of openness and collegiality and suggest "Let's just take Karen's suggestion first and then move onto Darren's. Would our new staff members be able to do that work?"

f.   Ask open questions, maintain energy

As the discussion moves on through the issues, you continue to ask open questions and paraphrase what people have said – noting the best suggestions as you go. Some people become frustrated at how long it is taking. You continue to emphasize that there are solutions to the problems: "It's just about carrying on considering all the possibilities."

Maxine has been very quiet again. You see an opportunity to hear a different perspective. "You've been very quiet - what do you think Maxine?" Maxine mentions that she had done some change management in her previous role and had begun working on documenting a more efficient change management sign-off process. She has been too busy to do much on it, but she thinks that there is a much better way.

After much robust discussion you have a list of possible solutions – some are short term and others will take longer.

Short term

Allocate the 2 new staff to work on the documentation backlog

Seek increased payment for after-hours work

Propose the rollout of fast access to the secure network

<u>Long term</u>

Develop proposal for overhaul of Network

Seek opportunities to move between the Network and the Server groups to provide stall swap opportunities or cross training to assist each other with projects and busy times.

Propose a more efficient change management sign-off process

Cut out the consultants and deal directly with the rail company

Stage Four: Considering Solutions

Once again you suggest a short break before moving into considering which solutions would be the best investment and provide the best results. You ask everyone to come back prepared to discuss the advantages and disadvantages of each possible solution. When you reconvene, you ask what external factors might be relevant.

g.   Consider external factors: risks, synergies etc.

Because many of the solutions require cooperation from other teams, the consulting company and the client, there a relevant external factors and potential synergies. You note each of the parties that may want some input into the solution. There are also risks, particularly if something goes wrong with Networks based on a change you are proposing. You note the extent of the risks, their likelihood and some ideas for mitigation. The meeting agrees that the idea of developing a proposal for an overhaul of Network should be dropped for now. There would be a lot of work involved and the consulting company are already doing an overhaul and are unlikely to welcome an alternative proposal. You suggest that the two new staff might resent being stuck on the documentation and ask if there is a way to spread it out among the team. Adrienne says that she would be happy to look at how it could be split up in such a way that everyone does some of the backlog.

The idea of cutting out the consulting company, given they currently have the contract, is likely to be sensitive, so you remove it from the list and undertake to raise it informally with Ken.

h.   Identify a small-scale test

Two of the solutions could be attempted on a small scale first. You undertake to speak to your colleague Rob, who manages the Network group, to see if they are open to exchanging one staff member on a trial basis. Similarly, the after-hours work could be the place to try a faster secure access system. Darren volunteers to put together a protocol showing how it would work, and the advantages.

i.   Make 'who is doing what' clear, including deadlines

You have a number of things that can be tried and so you finalize the solutions with the actions and dates as follows:

Short term

You are to speak to the new staff about helping with the documentation backlog, by close of business Friday. Adrienne to split up the backlog and provide it to you by next Wednesday.

George will speak to the human resources representative and ask them to look at similar allowances in other parts of the business and write a proposal that our team receive the same amount by next Wednesday.

Darren to deliver the protocol and proposal for fast access to the secure network by next Wednesday.

Long term

You to speak to Rob about exchanging one staff member on a trial basis by next Wednesday.

Maxine to meet with Pina and Luis to explain the more efficient change management sign-off process. All three to prioritize documenting it. Draft to be discussed at next month's team meeting.

j.   Values check

As you usually do, you ask one last question – given our team and company values 'should we do this?' Naimh raises the additional work that has come out of the meeting. "Given we're already overstretched, won't this just add to the problem?" You undertake to speak to Ken about some temporary additional support to get through this next month.

Stage Five: Document

At the end of the day, you send the whole team an email, thanking everyone for their contributions – whether in the meeting, or covering the work so that the meeting could go ahead. You list the tasks and the due dates. Finally, you offer support if anyone wants to chat about the tasks they have been given or if they encounter any obstacles.

The next day you meet with Ken to go over the complaints and possible solutions, while also pointing out the contribution that the consulting company is making to the delays. You also arrange to talk to two of your team members one to one. First you meet with Darren to discuss his tendency to dominate in meetings, and his critique of Karen's idea. After you explain the importance of hearing from everyone, he agrees to try listening more in future meetings. Next you meet with Maxine about her tendency not to participate until asked, when she has great insights to offer. After you explain the importance of hearing from everyone, she agrees to try to offer her ideas more in future meetings.

What happened?

Three months later you have all of the solutions in place, the new change management sign-off process, the faster secure access and the increased after-hours allowance mean that the complaints have ceased. The team is less stressed as there were more people rostered on after hours. For the last month they have also had the opportunity to apply to work in the Server group, increasing their knowledge and skills. One of your team is over in Networks on a rotation and there are two others ready to take future rotations. Ken is very happy that the client is happy. He is also relieved that the danger of losing big amounts of money is much lower than the whole time he has been in the role.

Conclusion

The challenges we have covered in this chapter tend to be amplified by increased rate of change affecting every workplace. Bigger changes and less time to respond to them means that can be a lack of clarity about all the factors that may be involved in a decision. However, the principles we have discussed are helpful in this situation too. Sometimes all that you can do is acknowledge that you don't have all the information you would like, decide on a small step forward, and have a plan if things go wrong. Then you are not paralysed by indecision. You can gather more information from each small step and you can review what you have learned before moving onto the next.

This chapter has provided some practical guidance that helps to illustrate how the various elements of good character come into play. By involving your team in decision making, you are demonstrating vulnerability – not claiming to have all the answers. You are laying out the challenge in front of the team honestly. You are communicating well, by providing the background to a situation and by being open to the views of your team, getting their input. You are also asking open questions and helping your team to build on any ideas offered. You show that you trust your team through delegation.[47] You are showing your confidence in their abilities. You are consistent in being prepared to support them. You are giving them an opportunity to make their own mistakes and learn from them. You are allowing them to grow in their capacity to make decisions and to manage tasks with an eye to the bigger picture. You are giving them the opportunity to progress in their own careers. As we will discuss in the next chapter, you are doing your best to be a role model of good management!

Start your journey with just 5 minutes a day

See suggestions below:

Day 1: Reflect on your strengths and weaknesses in decision making.

Day 2: Choose one thing from this chapter to try today that would improve on one thing from your Day 1 reflection.

Day 3: Reflect on your discussions with your team. Do you encourage a diversity of ideas (for example)?

Day 4: Choose one thing from this chapter to try today that would improve on one thing from your Day 3 reflection.

Day 5: Reflect on what you have learned from trying these things. Are there any lessons to learn? What can you do next week?

Chapter 9:
Conclusion – Being an Inspiration

©dominicmcloughlin.com

<u>In this Chapter:</u>

- The best manager ever

https://dominicmcloughlin.com/

This book is intended to help you be a manager that people will one day refer to as the 'best manager I ever had'. As we have seen, this is a journey rather than an instant fix. The final finding from the survey (referenced throughout this book) relates to overcoming difficulties. When thinking of the best managers, 83% (975) said that they overcame difficulties. When thinking of the worst managers, only 17% (200) overcame difficulties.[48] This ongoing effort to improve and to overcome the various obstacles that managers face is another critical element of being an excellent manager. If we think about all the challenges facing a manager, it is easy to see why this attribute is also important.

Many people who are good at their job are promoted to manage a team of people doing the work that they were previously doing. However, far too often, there is not enough guidance or assistance provided in making this adjustment. The role of the manager is different in many important ways and requires time for thinking and reflection, which is often scarce. You must make time to think about what is coming next month or what might be coming up next year. You have to spend time thinking about how your team works. Who fits best for each available role? Where will replacement staff come from? What knowledge and skills need to be built up now, so that they are available when they are needed next year? How does your team interact with other parts of the organization?

Your team, your organization and your clients all have expectations of your role. You need to develop an awareness around how you interact, what your various stakeholders want or need from you. You also need to have high expectations. Your team will rise to a bar that is set high, but only when they trust you and feel supported to achieve it. There is a view that part of a manager's role is to take the heat from above and defend the people who work for you. However, this cannot stop you from expecting personal responsibility. What you want to do is to help them embrace responsibility, to grow and develop as a person and as a professional. By giving people challenging tasks and projects, you can help to build resilience in the face of difficulties and patience.

The best managers led by example. They modeled the expected behaviors. They were people of good character and known to be honest and ethical. They would not delegate a task that they were not willing to do themselves. It is worth remembering that most of your team want to know whether you are capable of delivering, and whether you have good intentions toward them.[49] Having developed a reputation for learning from mistakes, honesty and having the good of the team as a primary goal, you have a solid basis for ensuring your communication, decision making and delegation skills build trust and outstanding performance.

As one survey respondent put it:

"The best manager I ever had… You knew where you stood with them… Very understanding but firm… Treated you as an equal… Gave me an opportunity to develop myself professionally, without being concerned that I may one day threaten their position"

So, it turns out that the best manager people ever had is probably similar to the manager we would all like to have. Someone who learns from their mistakes and allows others to learn from theirs. Someone who is good at their job, but recognizes that their main role is to facilitate the success of the team and looks for ways to develop the people working with them. Someone who is honest and consistent. Someone who communicates well – clearly, openly, honestly and in ways that are easily understood. Someone who keeps the team goal in people's minds, motivating them. Someone who involves the team in decision making and delegating work appropriately. Someone who overcomes the inevitable difficulties in any workplace.

This someone is you.

Continue your journey

By now you know what you can do in just 5 minutes a day. However, there is a lot to consider and many things to try.

Every Day: Reflect on a specific area

Every Other Day: Try to improve it

Once a Week: Learn the lessons

Keep going!

If you liked this book, I would be grateful if you left a review – I read them all – and I use your feedback to improve the book and my courses. See the next page for your free course.

FREE GIFT FOR MY READERS

How To Be a Better Manager, in JUST 5 Minutes a Day!

Get your Free Starter Kit here:
https://dominicmcloughlin.com/free-starter-kit/

Getting started is often the hardest part. However, as soon as you get going and the momentum kicks in, you can be unstoppable.

Therefore, I created this FREE Starter Kit to help you – in just 5 minutes a day!

Inside this FREE Starter Kit are:
- 5 tutorial videos
- 5 downloadable workbooks

Each Video has ideas for 5 minutes a day for one working week!

Find the answer to ALL of the following people management questions:
- How do I find more time?
- How do I develop a manager's mindset?
- How do I build my people skills?
- How do I understand who my clients are?
- How do I build my team culture?

Over one month of ideas to help you improve!

About the Author

With 20 years' experience in Leadership and People Management, Dr Dominic McLoughlin began his career in the high conflict area of Industrial Relations. Moving into People Management to help prevent issues from arising, Dominic has helped clients in many different industries, including IT, finance, retail and education.

Dominic undertook his PhD at UNSW, researching the importance of integrity and character in management behaviour for building trust within organisations. Dominic also has 20 years' experience teaching and facilitating a diverse range of university courses on people management. He currently delivers programs at the AGSM, Western Sydney University and his own business.

Dominic is a Fellow of the Institute of Managers and Leaders, the Australian Human Resources Institute, the Higher Education Academy and the Chartered Institute for Personnel and Development. In addition to his PhD, Dominic has a Bachelor of Commerce, a Master of Business from the University of Technology Sydney, and a number of publications.

Dominic works with managers at all levels to improve the management of their people.

Connect With Me

Email: dominic@dominicmcloughlin.com
Facebook Page: https://www.facebook.com/McLoughlinDominic
LinkedIn: https://www.linkedin.com/in/dr-dominic-mcloughlin-15a3573/
Get your Free Starter Kit here:
https://dominicmcloughlin.com/free-starter-kit/

Endnotes/References

[1] The 'lack of trust' is such a fundamental problem that it forms the first layer in Lencioni's famous book: Patrick M. Lencioni (2002) *The Five Dysfunctions of a Team: A Leadership Fable*, Jossey-Bass, San Francisco

[2] This was an analysis of 106 Studies, 27,103 individuals - see Dirks and Ferrin (2002) "Trust in Leadership: Meta-Analytic Findings and Implications for Research and Practice" *Journal of Applied Psychology*, Vol. 87, No. 4, 611–628.

[3] Similarly, a 2017 Harvard Business Review article on the neuroscience of trust reports that employees in high-trust organizations are more productive, collaborate better, stay longer and are happier. All of this eventually drives stronger performance. Paul J. Zak, "The Neuroscience of Trust", *Harvard Business Review,* Jan–Feb 2017 pp85-90

[4] We will go on to explore this, but see for example these two books: Sison (2003) *The Moral Capital of Leaders Why Virtue Matters:* https://www.amazon.com/Moral-Capital-Leaders-Horizons-Leadership/dp/1843760460 also Harvard (2007) *Virtuous Leadership: https://www.amazon.com/VIRTUOUS-LEADERSHIP-Alexandre-Havard/dp/1594172048*

[5] Dirks and Ferrin (2002) "Trust in Leadership: Meta-Analytic Findings and Implications for Research and Practice" *Journal of Applied Psychology*, Vol. 87, No. 4, 611–628.

[6] McLoughlin, D (2014) *Knowledge Worker Trust Within Organisations*, Sydney, Ithikos Pty Ltd

[7] Covey, S. R. (1989) *The seven habits of highly effective people: Restoring the character ethic*, New York, Simon and Schuster

[8] Berkowitz, M and Fekula, M (1999) "Educating for character", *About Campus* Nov- Dec 1999, 17.

[9] Chinchilla, Nuria; Moragas, Maruja (2008) *Masters of Our Destiny*, University of Navarre, Navarre

[10] Good habits can be acquired through practice – we aren't born with them – we develop them. Chinchilla, Nuria; Moragas, Maruja (2008) *Masters of Our Destiny*, University of Navarre, Navarre

[11] See for example: Wadhwa, H (2022) "Small Actions Make Great Leaders" *Harvard Business Review*: https://hbr.org/2022/06/small-actions-make-great-leaders

[12] Dweck, C. S. (2006). *Mindset: The New Psychology of Success*. New York: Random House

[13] Beck, R and Harter, J "Why Good Managers Are So Rare" *Harvard Business Review*, March 2014 – reporting Gallup research: https://hbr.org/2014/03/why-good-managers-are-so-rare

[14] McLoughlin, D (2014) *Knowledge Worker Trust Within Organisations*, Sydney, Ithikos Pty Ltd

[15] Using QSR NVivo

[16] Lei, Y; Minya, X; Pellegrini, E (2021) "The Boss's Long Arm: The Differential Impact of Authoritarian and Benevolent Leadership on Spousal Family Satisfaction" *Frontiers in Psychology*, Vol.12: https://www.frontiersin.org/articles/10.3389/fpsyg.2021.780030/full

[17] "Many people who feel like impostors grew up in families that placed a big emphasis on achievement… In our society there's a huge pressure to achieve... There can be a lot of confusion between approval and love and worthiness. Self-worth becomes contingent on achieving." Weir, K (2013) *gradPSYCH* Vol. 11 No. 4.

[18] Turnover in your team has some obvious costs such as recruitment time and money and less efficiency while a new person learns the role. However, there are also hidden costs such as the time taken to conduct the interviews, the loss of motivation while everyone else picks up the slack, and the lack of focus on future challenges while we 'get through these few weeks'. Even harder to measure are the team upheaval, the effort required to form a new person in the 'way we do things' and the changed trust dynamics.

[19] If you are a trusted manager, good people want to stay, as they enjoy their work and their workplace. This saves you a lot of time and expense. This also allows you to focus on the things that really matter. In fact, often a trusted manager will be told in advance that someone is thinking about leaving. This means that you have time to change the person's mind or to craft a plan to allow them to be paid more or promoted within your organization – not losing them at all.

[20] See Chapter 2.

[21] 'What is good leadership?' (1998:13), where the "… use of the word

good here has two senses, morally good and technically good or effective" (Ciulla, 1998: 13). Ciulla, J. (1998). Leadership Ethics: Mapping the Territory. *Ethics, The Heart of Leadership*. J. Ciulla. Westport, Greenwood Publishing Group, Inc.

"Finally, it is widely recognized that trust is an important concept in organizations, but there is rarely any mention of where it comes from. Moral trust comes from an appraisal of the manager's or leader's moral character. For example, to be trusted a manager should be honest (Locke, 2003:434)." Locke, E. (2003), "Good Definitions: The Epistemological Foundation of Scientific Progress" *Organizational Behavior: The State of The Science*, J. Geenberg. Mahwah, New Jersey, Lawrence Erlbaum Associates.

[22] Miller. B and West, R (Ed) (2020) *Integrity, Honesty, and Truth Seeking*, Oxford, Oxford University Press

[23] This not only saves you time in finding out what's really going on, it also means that your decision making is better informed. Furthermore, when describing the current 'state of affairs' to your own manager, you can have more confidence that you are correct.

[24] Sometimes destructive gossip is a symptom of a serious problem where a 'whistleblower' is needed. Here we aren't talking about that, but rather unfounded, destructive gossip and dysfunctional working relationships

[25] McLoughlin, D (2014) *Knowledge Worker Trust Within Organisations*, Sydney, Ithikos Pty Ltd

[26] McLoughlin, D (2014) *Knowledge Worker Trust Within Organisations*, Sydney, Ithikos Pty Ltd

[27] Dool, R., & Alam, T. (2022) *Change Fatigue Revisited: A New Framework for Leading Change,* Business Expert Press.

[28] Development Dimensions International's Global Leadership Forecast 2021, p.25: https://www.ddiworld.com/global-leadership-forecast-2021

[29] Development Dimensions International's Global Leadership Forecast 2021, p.24: https://www.ddiworld.com/global-leadership-forecast-2021

[30] Covey, S. R. (1989) *The seven habits of highly effective people: Restoring the character ethic*, New York, Simon and Schuster

[31] Kahn, W (1990) "Psychological Conditions of Personal Engagement and Disengagement at Work", *Academy of Management Journal*. 33 (4): 692–724

[32] Edmondson, A (1999). "Psychological Safety and Learning Behavior in Work Teams" *Administrative Science Quarterly*, 44 (2): 350–383.

[33] If you put 'Manager as Coach' into Amazon, you will get more than 370 books

[34] Hudson, N (2002) "Lighten the darkness: Personality interventions targeting agreeableness also reduce participants' levels of the dark triad", *Journal of Personality,* 00, 1-6

[35] Some authors refer to humility rather than vulnerability – see for example: Jim Collins (2001) "Level 5 Leadership: The Triumph of Humility and Fierce Resolve", *Harvard Business Review*
https://hbr.org/2001/01/level-5-leadership-the-triumph-of-humility-and-fierce-resolve-2

[36] See for example: Nagraj, D (2022) Virtual Leadership: Understanding The Communication Styles Needed For Leadership In A Virtual World: https://www.forbes.com/sites/forbescommunicationscouncil/2022/07/13/virtual-leadership-understanding-the-communication-styles-needed-for-leadership-in-a-virtual-world/amp/

[37] A 2015 Gallup study found that CEOs who excel in delegating generate 33 percent higher revenue: https://news.gallup.com/businessjournal/182414/delegating-huge-management-challenge-entrepreneurs.aspx

[38] For more information about micromanagement, see this online article: Popov, I (2022) "Why You Need to Stop Micromanaging Your Team and Learn to Let Go", *Entrepreneur*: https://www.entrepreneur.com/article/429048

[39] See Chapter 2.

[40] Guinot, Monfort, and Chiva (2021) "How to Increase Job Satisfaction: The Role of Participative Decisions and Feeling Trusted", *Employee Relations,* Vol 43, No.6:1397–1413

[41] If you put 'Decision Making' into Amazon, you will get more than 20,00 books.

[42] Ned Herrmann (1990) *The Creative Brain*, Brain Books, Lake Lure, North Carolina.

[43] The stages can all occur quickly – in a two-hour meeting, for example. With more complex decisions, there may be gaps between the phases of a day or two, sometimes even longer.

[44] A useful example is the WRAP model - see Heath, C; Heath D (2013) *Decisive: How to Make Better Choices in Life and Work,* Canada, Random House https://heathbrothers.com/wp-content/uploads/2013/03/The_WRAP_Process_one_pager.pdf

[45] Of course, you cannot just allow the loudest voices to determine your decision, so ensuring you hear from everyone in your team is very important.

[46] See Chapter 2.

[47] Steven Covey (Jr) suggests that leaders who have become more trustworthy can struggle to be sufficiently trusting. Covey, SMR (2022) *Trust and Inspire: How Truly Great Leaders Unleash Greatness in Others*, Simon & Schuster.

[48] See Chapter 2.

[49] Cuddy, A; Kohut, M; Nelftnger, J (2013) "Connect, Then Lead" *Harvard Business Review* Vol. 3, July-August 2013, also Ciulla's observation that: "good leadership… has two senses, morally good and technically good or effective". Ciulla, J. (1998) "Leadership Ethics: Mapping the Territory" *Ethics, The Heart of Leadership*, Westport, Greenwood Publishing Group, Inc. p.13

Connect With Me

Email: dominic@dominicmcloughlin.com
Facebook Page: https://www.facebook.com/McLoughlinDominic
LinkedIn: https://www.linkedin.com/in/dr-dominic-mcloughlin-15a3573/

Get your Free Starter Kit here:
https://dominicmcloughlin.com/free-starter-kit/

Made in the USA
Las Vegas, NV
04 December 2023